MY BROTHER, LECH WALESA

MY BROTHER, LECH WALESA

by

Walter Brolewicz

With an Introduction by Lech Walesa

TRiBECA
COMMUNICATIONS, INC.
New York

ISBN 0-943392-52-7

Written by Walter Brolewicz

Distributed in Canada by Prentice-Hall Canada Inc., 1870 Birchmount Road, Scarborough,
Ontario M1P 2J7

Photos on the following pages provided by Black Star:
18, 20, 22, 34, 35, 37, 38, 44, 45, 56, 57, 58, 72, 73, 74, 75, 76, 77, 90, 91, 92, 93, 94, 95, 98,
112, 113, 118, 119, 126, 135, 136, 152, 153, 154, 156, 158.

Photos on these pages provided by World Wide Photos:
19, 21, 23, 70, 71.

Photos on the following pages from this author's collection:
12, 33, 41, 42, 43, 50, 54, 57, 62, 66,85, 102, 103, 109, 110, 115, 117, 121, 122, 125, 127, 155,
160.

Typography by Times Printing, Kingston, Pa.

Printed in the United States of America
First Edition.

1 2 3 4 5 6 7 8 9 10

DEDICATION

Dla Leszka
Z nadzieja o lepsze jutro

To Lech,
With hope for a better tomorrow

ACKNOWLEDGEMENTS

The author would like to thank Henry Buklad for his encouragement to get a book out of me, and to David Cohn, Jim Mann, Lisa Marsoli and Gerri Santaniello for all their efforts to finish this book under a great deal of pressure.

CONTENTS

FOREWORD

I am, by profession, an engineer, a man who likes to talk and write on technical matters. I have never before written about a non-technical subject, let alone about a man who is known the world over.

Lech Walesa is indeed an international figure. Winner of the Nobel Peace Prize in 1983, he is a leader and a symbol, not only in his own beloved Poland but to the rest of the world as well.

It was, of course, not always so. Lech Walesa, his five brothers and his sister were relatively unknown, even to me, their cousin, until 1947. It was then that I began to address bundles from my mother to the Walesa family in Poland. I had known that I had cousins in Poland, but it wasn't until 1947, when Poland had become desperate in its need for food, clothing, and medicine that my family became an important part of their lives. During World War II, Poland had been devastated. Lech Walesa's family, like many others, was split up when his father became interned in a German work camp. Shortly after the war, Lech's father died as a result of the deprivations he had endured. His mother, my aunt, then married Stanley Walesa, her husband's brother. Stanley had made a promise to his dying brother that he would care for his widow and their four children, Izabela, Edward, Stanley, and Lech.

And so, Stanley Walesa, Lech's uncle and mine, became Lech's stepfather and the father of Lech's half brothers, Tadeusz, Zygmunt, and Wojciech.

Throughout those years, my mother, Janina (who had come to America with my father in the early 1900's), helped to provide for the many needs of her relatives still in Poland by sending sweaters, coats, canned goods, medicine, shoes—whatever would travel—to her sister. This was a common practice among Poles in America. And for years, I remembered "Walesa" as a name I would write on heavy bundles that I would then, at my mother's command, bring directly to the post office to send to my "cousins" in Poland.

In 1971, Lech's mother and her husband Stanley came to America at my mother's invitation. By then their children were all grown and Lech was an electrician in the Gdansk shipyards. That year Poland was seized by events that commanded world attention and showed its willingness to endure and resist, a willingness that often erupted into world headlines.

But here in America, in Jersey City, New Jersey, Lech's mother and his stepfather, Stanley and Feliska, were looking for work, living with my mother, and already planning for the day when, having earned enough credit for social security, they could return to Poland.

Less than five years later, Lech's mother died, hit by a car in 1975 as she crossed a street near her home. Lech's stepfather, my uncle Stanley, remained in Jersey City, close to his only family in this country, my mother.

In 1980, Lech Walesa became known to all the world. Since then, my own world has never been far removed from that name. Stanley Walesa, while he was still alive, was often asked to make appearances at various functions. He had never mastered English and I would often accompany him as his translator. As Lech's cousin, I too had my share of invitations to attend meetings, dinners, and other functions as well.

And so what had begun as a trip to the post office with a bundle of old clothing had developed into an increasingly frequent series of appearances, engagements, and interviews. There was correspondence and communication with Lech in Poland, even an occasional telephone call. To a small but growing circle of associates and supporters here in the United States, Stanley Walesa and I had become a link to Lech.

When Stanley died in August 1981, I was appointed administrator of his estate. With that there were other communications that were necessary, communications which led to the two journeys I have now made to Poland, one in December 1982 and the other in March 1983.

On these trips, I stayed with Lech and his family as well as with other Walesa family members, and witnessed, as did much of the world, the events that took place while I was there. Lech has always been an extremely open man. He has always been willing to express his views and has always asked that they be made known. He is a great man, but he does not do these things to add to his own greatness. He does these things only to serve the cause of the people of Poland.

Just as I witnessed the events that have filled newsreels, magazines, and other media, I have also witnessed moments when the door of Lech's apartment finally closed to the rest of the world and the phone linking him to the workers of Poland finally sat quiet and unused on the table. I cannot and do not claim to have any special insights into this man, or any special qualifications to convey what I have seen and heard. It is my hope that what I write will be of interest to those who will read it, and will be of some usefulness in the efforts of Lech Walesa and his colleagues.

I must make clear that I do not speak for Lech. Even those times when he asks me to convey his thoughts or a message to a group of his supporters here in America, I do not truly speak for him. Only he can do that and I would not be so bold as to assume that I can be other than an imperfect messenger.

It was after my first trip to Poland with my brother Henry in 1982 that I decided to write about my experience. But, pressures from my regular job never allowed me to even begin. It was not until my next trip, in March 1983, that I began to make any progress along these lines. I had Lech's encouragement, and I began to take a few notes in a small diary that I kept during this second visit. I began to make more detailed notes of my experiences and conversations with Lech during the seven and one-half hour return flight home. There was never any question in my mind that I should not make tapes of any conversations with Lech, or take any detailed notes while I was still in the country with him; I had to rely mostly on my memory.

Writing about Lech is not easy. It is difficult to describe someone who, while in your company, leaps into your heart and your brain and seems to sense immediately what makes you tick. You find yourself mesmerized by his presence. He is able to reduce an argument or a problem to its simplest components. And so I accepted the challenge of writing about Lech, but not without many reservations. As fluent as my Polish is, translation is not an exact science, especially as I have had to rely so much on memory. But I can still hear his words, "Do it, but with some caution. Don't pin any labels on me. No one can write my words, but just come as close as you can. Don't embarrass or

insult anyone, but let people know about the life and spirit here. Make sure they don't forget us."

A word about the title of this book. Lech and I are cousins because our mothers were sisters. However, in Poland the term "cousin" is considered too remote to be used among close family, and is normally used to designate a blood relationship in a somewhat technical manner. The word brother, in addition to its established meaning, is used in Poland to mean something like family. It denotes a more intimate relationship than the broad use of "brother" in English, as in "the brotherhood of man." Lech insisted, upon my arrival in Poland for my first visit with him, that we thereafter refer to ourselves as brothers and that I do away with the "technical" term cousin I had been using before, a usage he claimed too remote to suit him. I was, of course, honored by this. He was kind enough to add that my failure to refer to him as 'my brother' had hurt his feelings.

Whatever the nuance is of language, whatever his generosity in wishing me well, and whatever my own failings, I feel privileged to have this opportunity to write about "my brother, Lech."

INTRODUCTION

My brother has asked me to supply an introduction to this book. I am reluctant to do so because I may never see the translation before print. I am cautious and wary and leery about people who put words in my mouth. No one will write my book or thoughts for me until I do it myself.

But I have given my brother my support and encouragement for this book of his travels in Poland and conversations we had together. We had many. We touched on politics and human feelings. I shared my thoughts with him.

I have been asked what kind of leader's hat I wear.

My hat will always be a worker's hat and it will always hang on a nail. It's a leader's hat but it shall always be a common hat, used by common people for common purposes. It shall always hang on a nail to remind me or anyone else that I am not endowed with superior wisdom, and that it can be worn by anyone for the common good. Anyone who insists on wearing such a hat on his head because he thinks he is ordained by God tends to corrupt himself with the power of such a hat. Someone once said "Power tends to corrupt, and absolute power corrupts absolutely." I believe that.

I also believe that with power there is always a desire for more power. Those who have it will usually find ways to get more of it. So far as I can see, the history of all governments is pretty much a history of men wearing their crowns too long, with too much power, seeking more power.

I am reluctant to wear even the common hat of a leader. But until someone else comes along I will at least take it and hang it on a common nail. It will be there to remind me of the potential corruption it invites.

Lech Walesa
March 1983

CHAPTER 1
GOING HOME

It was December 5, 1982. The time was 1:30 p.m. The place was Gdansk, Poland. I got out of a four-door Skoda and set my feet on the ground in front of a drab apartment building, part of a complex of post World War II apartments known as the *Zaspa*. We were on the Street of Pilots and in front of me was the entrance to the building that is the home of Lech Walesa.

Even though we are first cousins, I was nervous and anxious about meeting this man. He was famous, a celebrity of international stature. His picture and story must have appeared in every newspaper in the world. He was a leader. He was a symbol. He was a man who seized history by the shoulder and shook it. Although I had been sending him letters, packages and telegrams for years, and we had spoken on the telephone, but had never met face to face before.

It had been a long journey to Lech's house. Crises in Poland, and the hectic months since August 1980, when Lech Walesa first made headlines, had intervened and kept us apart many times. Trips and meetings had been planned and then cancelled. The eleven months of his internment by the government delayed our meeting further. But the Polish government had finally approved my visa, right around the time of Lech's release in November 1982, and the day had been set when I would at last meet my famous cousin.

*Lech about to board a flight to Rome to
visit the Pope.*

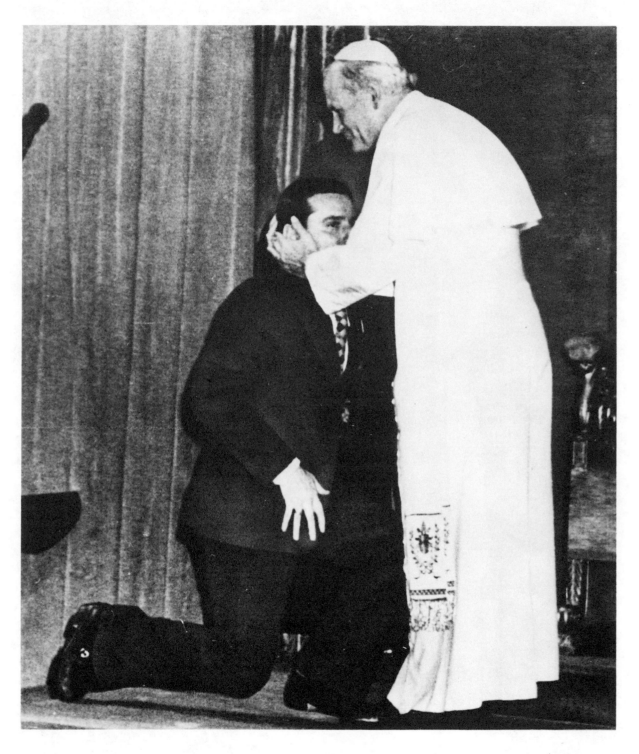

Pope John Paul II embraces Lech during an audience granted to members of the Solidarity movement at the Vatican.

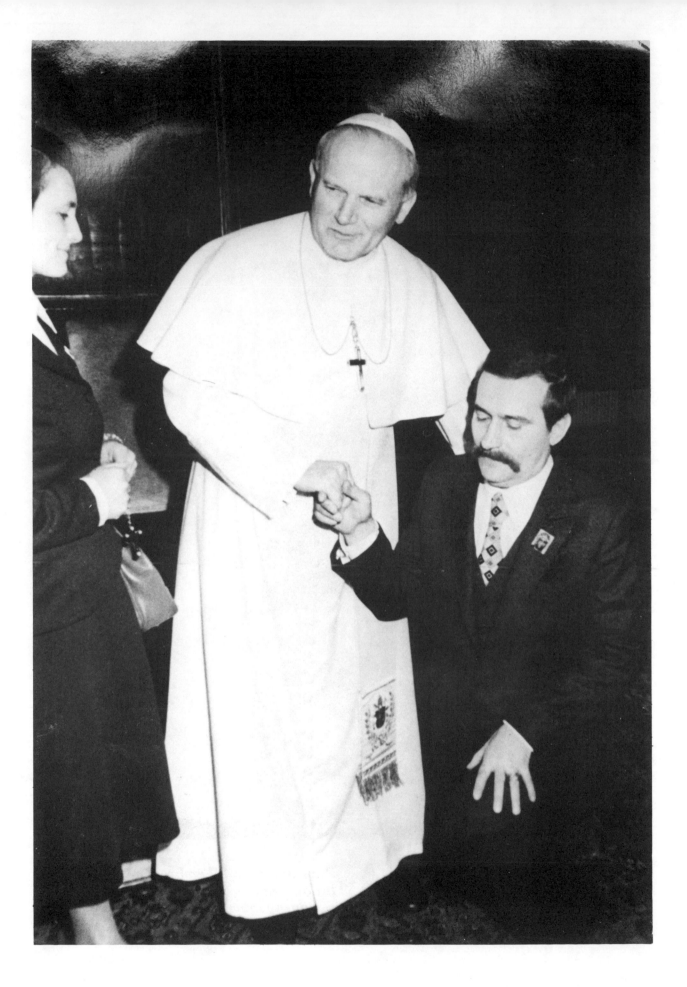

Lech presents Pope John Paul II with a replica of the workers' monument in Gdansk during a special audience at the Vatican.

Lech kneels to Pope John Paul II during the Solidarity leader's trip to Rome.

Lech visits the Nijo castle in Kyoto, Japan; it was once the home of the Tokugawa Dynasty.

*Lech speaks with 93-year-old economist
and founder of the Polish dissident group,
Edward Lipinski.*

And even that day was delayed. Scheduled originally for the week of November 20-27, 1982, the visit was put off by the last-minute decision of my brother, Henry Brolewicz, to accompany me. There was so much luggage, including the personal belongings of the Walesa family, that my brother insisted on coming along to give me extra security and help.

I had previously been appointed, as the closest blood relative, to serve as the administrator of the estate of Lech's stepfather, who, for the last ten years of his life, had lived in Jersey City, New Jersey and had died in 1981, just as he was planning his return to Poland. As the administrator of his estate, I was now going to Poland myself to take some of the property of his estate to the Walesa family.

Finally, we arrived at Kennedy Airport. My brother and I were dressed for winter even though, in New York, it was the hottest December we could remember. We felt apprehensive even as we boarded the plane. We were about to go to the roots of our heritage, to the home our own parents had left behind many years before, and to visit our now famous relative for the first time.

Our flight seemed an eternity, many hours and thousands of miles. But after a stop-over at Frankfurt to change planes, we were, it seemed, suddenly and at last setting foot on Polish soil. We sniffed the crisp thirty-degree air, looked at the sun, and tested the firmness of the ground. It was wonderful. I looked across the flat terrain and saw armed militiamen, rifles slung on their shoulders, watching us. It was the Poland of our family ties, but it was also the Poland of martial law.

We were directed to a customs control section. We got in line for the first customs check where a uniformed man was to inspect our passports and visas. The people ahead of me seemed to be processed through fairly rapidly, less than five minutes for each. Then it was our turn. Within a few seconds the man inside the booth made a phone call. A few seconds later another man came to the booth and there was a conference. Suddenly, a third and then a fourth man were standing near us. The atmosphere became tense. We were nervous, but it was exciting as well. The senior official noted that my visa listed Lech Walesa as one of the people I was to visit. To the best of my knowledge, my brother and I were the first foreigners permitted to visit Lech since his release by the government after the eleven month internment.

We were finally approved and then sent to a customs agent for baggage inspection. When all our baggage was collected, we were directed to a line with only one traveler ahead of us. Five minutes later we were moved to another line with four people in it and, after fifteen minutes, to still a third line, also with four others ahead of us.

While all this was going on, I kept looking for a familiar face on the other side of the partition. I had wired Lech's sister, Izabela Mlynska, to meet us at the airport. Never having met Iza before, I had only my recollection of a four-year old photograph of her to guide me. Then I spotted her across the room, waving one hand and clutching a bouquet of flowers in the other. My eyes filled with tears. She bore such a strong resemblance to my own mother, that I could not believe it.

Finally, it was our turn at customs. Once again my visa was reviewed. It became apparent there would be some delay. My first bag was opened and I declared what I had. The customs agent, blond and attractive, insisted on poking into everything. In a moment her supervisor was hovering over her, carefully watching the whole process. I began to get upset. Bag by bag each item was scrutinized with what I thought was an excess of thoroughness. The room was now almost deserted, the other passengers all having cleared through.

Four tape cassettes I had brought containing selections from Mozart, Bach, Chopin, and Beethoven, favorites of mine, were uncovered and became the objects of an intense debate. The agents were suspicious and would not be reassured—the tapes were to be confiscated. I put up a fuss, insisted that they should listen to excerpts and let them clear. But the agents insisted otherwise. Two more officials got into the act. My brother cautioned me in English that I was getting arrogant and my attitude was likely to get us into trouble. He quickly convinced me to cooperate and release the tapes. I took the receipt they gave me and they promised that I could pick the cassettes up within two days, after they had been reviewed.

Then came another delay. We were directed to a private room where the agents insisted on counting all of our money. By the time they were satisfied with everything, almost two hours had passed, it was now the middle of the afternoon. We were finally repacked and approved for release. Iza and her husband, Bronek, were still waiting, standing alone in the large reception room. There were tears and kisses and that beautiful Polish custom of greeting with flowers. It touched us both deeply. We were among family and in Poland.

Warsaw had had a little snow that day, and it was a cloudy afternoon. But it was a pleasure to feel the clean cool air after an unseasonably hot New York.

We started out for Sochaczew, Iza's hometown. Despite our experience at the airport, I had the feeling the trip with Iza and Bronek was a new beginning, and a good one.

Once in the car, it was hard to keep up the conversation and catch all the sights at the same time. I kept looking out the window. I did not want to miss anything. My parents' beloved Poland, a thousand years of history, many wars—and it was still beautiful. There were black crows everywhere. Bronek told us the current joke in Poland. "They're Russian spies and report to the Kremlin."

We arrived at Bronek and Iza's house and there we had our first of many Polish meals. There was hot chicken broth, cooked ham, boiled potatoes, cheese and rye bread. I know that Iza and Bronek and their children had denied themselves much of the meager ration of food normally available to Poles just so they could stock up and feel prepared for our visit. Food shortages in Poland are very real. But Poles see in the sharing of a meal the essence of hospitality. It is impossible to enter the home of any Pole, as his guest, and not be virtually required to eat. And so, everywhere we went, every new friendship, every renewed acquaintance seemed to lead to another meal. This first meal at Iza's took a long time to finish because of our endless chatter about life in our respective countries.

They were well off enough to have comfortable furniture, a collection of china, and some attractive crystal pieces. Their apartment had portraits of family and friends and the religious icons found in most Polish homes. They even had a black and white TV set. There were only two channels, both government owned, and programming consisted mostly of news, documentaries, and lackluster talk shows. Our first night was pleasant, with our hosts seeing to it that every gesture of hospitality was extended to us both.

The next day we rented a car, a green Skoda, from Iza's neighbor, to drive to Gdansk, the home of Lech Walesa. We began the 146-mile drive with much anticipation. Bronek was our driver while Iza served as our guide. The countryside was more lush than I expected—broad fields and fertile black earth plowed under for the winter. We saw many older buildings, their architecture reflecting patterns and designs used in Poland for centuries. Many buildings, even those built more recently, seemed poorly maintained. The roads were surprisingly smooth and well maintained. All at once I wanted to embrace everything, the earth, the buildings, even the sky. This was a land worth loving and worth fighting for. The air was rich with its history. The towering trees that lined the road and the endless fertile fields beyond captured us and commanded our allegiance in a way no army could diminish or control. Poland—a nation of people tied for a thousand years to this land. Our parents' recollections, as they had told us many times when we were young, came alive. We passed through Plock, where my mother was raised; the city of Torun (Copernicus' home); Wloclawek (larger than I would have thought); Nowe (large and ancient as well, despite its name—Polish for "new").

As we continued, Bronek started to look worried. The Skoda was getting low on oil, and the gas stations, few and far between, had none to sell. Now the flocks of black crows that were everywhere seemed more ominous than before, and only added to our anxiety.

On the outskirts of Gdansk, I expressed some reservations to Hank about our meeting with Lech. After all, Lech was a man who had already met generals and presidents, dignitaries from Italy, France, Japan—and the Pope himself. Tens of thousands of workers had shaken his hand. I seriously wondered what his reaction would be. Would he be bored with this simple family reunion? Would he be too busy or too preoccupied to relax and talk about relatively insignificant family matters? Would there be room for us? Would we be an imposition? Would something in our chemistries clash? These questions and others were all on my mind as the car turned into the Street of Pilots and we parked in front of Lech's building.

Iza and Bronek noticed one of the children at the window, looking down at us. Hank and I debated who should be first at the door. We hurried up one flight of stairs and I pushed the doorbell. In an instant the door was flung open and there was a wild yell from inside: "They're here, they're here!" Standing in the doorway was Lech himself, arms thrown wide, having to almost shout above the family racket, "Welcome, brothers, welcome. Come in, please, come in."

Our eyes met. We embraced and then exchanged the traditional greeting, a kiss to the cheek, first to one cheek, then the other, then back again. I stuttered the Polish blessing, "God love you and all in this house." Lech answered at once, "My brother, God must love us to make this meeting possible. My home and all in it are yours."

Lech turned to Hank, "We are so happy you arrived safely, brother," he said. They embraced and Hank said, "God bless you, Lech," with great emotion. And then added, "Greetings from my mother and our family," followed by more kissing, one cheek and then the other, as before.

Lech's wife, Danuta, hung back shyly, then stepped forward. Lech introduced us, "My dearest, come meet my brothers from America." Hank tried another Polish greeting, kissing her hand, and then the embrace and kiss to each cheek.

We met some of the other members of the Walesa household. Four of the children were still in school, but three-year-old Magda and two-year-old Anna came shouting from another room to greet us. One-year-old Wiktoria watched the noisy scene from her walker.

Lech made other introductions. First there was the large figure of his bodyguard and friend, Henry by name, but known to everyone as "Dziadek," a Polish term of endearment meaning something like "Pop." Then Lech introduced us to his personal aide, Mieczyslaw (Mietek) Wachowski, a slender, bearded and courteous man, and then to Maciej Grzywaczewski, also an aide and his chauffeur as well.

We had already been in Lech's apartment for these few minutes when Lech turned to us and said, "Walter, you have made me very uncomfortable and somewhat sad." My heart skipped a beat. My God, I thought, what have I done to this man? I stammered saying, "Forgive me, but I don't understand."

"I have heard and seen you on the TV news before this was all brought to a halt, and in each case you consistently referred to me as 'cousin.' My 'cousin' this, my 'cousin' that. Don't you recognize the blood ties between us? Our mothers were sisters. In Poland, and certainly too with me, we are brothers."

I started to relax and said, "Lech, my cousin, excuse me, my brother, I thought that technically I was correct."

"Do you hear that, Danuta? 'technically' he said. Walter, that's rubbish. We must maintain our warmth and intimacy with family, and our love. From now on we are brothers. Do you understand? The same goes for you Henry. Understand?"

I could see Henry had also been a little tense. He embraced Lech and said, "I hear you, my brother."

I could not resist adding with a smile, "From now on, my cousin, we are brothers."

"Now, my brothers," Lech began, reaching for glasses of vodka that had been poured. "To our mothers and family!" There was a finality to that toast, a certainty that relaxed all of us as though things had now been set straight. We began to feel, enjoy, and delight in the charm and persuasiveness that we came to know as typical of Lech Walesa.

No sooner was our toasting complete than the kitchen table was filled with food and drink. I was astonished at the variety. Ham, salami, hot kielbasi and sauerkraut, rye bread, onions, pickles, cheese, butter, hot chicken soup, hot tea, vodka, and crackers; all in the tradition of Polish hospitality, a tradition that privation and difficulty had done little to diminish. As I was to learn later, Lech and his family received packages of food daily from supporters all over the world, both inside and outside of Poland. He keeps what he and his associates use and distributes the rest through the union organization or the church. The abundance of generosity shown by his supporters kept my brother and I well nourished throughout our stay.

Lech urged us to eat and then mentioned that we should see some of Gdansk before dark. He placed his car and Maciej at our disposal. "Eat lightly, now. Take a tour of the 'Old Town' section (a restoration of the older section of Gdansk) and come back for supper. We will talk more tonight," Lech said.

In a few minutes, Iza, Henry and I were off on our Gdansk tour. Bronek remained with Lech, and Maciej now became our driver and guide. Lech was cautious about coming with us anywhere during our two weeks in Poland. I learned later that even though he was considered a "free" man, he was something of a prisoner in his own house. He had been warned not to mingle with any crowds in violation of martial law. Yet it was difficult for him not to attract a crowd anywhere he went. Lech was not so much afraid of the repercussions for himself as he was of the consequences for the people greeting him.

CHAPTER 2
AT HOME WITH THE WALESAS

Gdansk itself was beautiful. The city center was filled with shoppers, strollers, and workers. A trolley line shuttled people back and forth. The "Old Town" reconstruction is something of a miracle too—I had seen photos of the World War II destruction.

With a history going back to 980 A.D., it is a city with thousand-year-old traditions. A seaport, previously known as Danzig (owing to former German control), it is an important industrial center, particularly for shipbuilding.

The name "Gdansk" is of Slavic origin, and the root "gd" appear in many words to designate swampy, marshy areas. Built on a low-lying delta of the Wisla River depression, its ancient marshes and swamps have been drained, filled in, and transformed into the pastures and fields that surround it.

Maciej took us down some historic streets and pointed out structures of great historical value. Here a house of artists, there a group of shops with antiques, all set in an informal atmosphere, as though yesterday were today. "We believe," Maciej began, "that Gdansk will someday be a tourist mecca. The restoration is slow because the money is lacking. People are amazing in Gdansk. They sense their history and they are willing to volunteer their service."

"When our Solidarity union was open and legal, there was talk that we would establish an independent fund to support this type of restoration. Just as Lech was part of many changes for workers' rights, he also promoted the establishment of a committee to document our history."

After our brief tour, we returned to Lech's house for supper—and many vodka toasts. We retired to the large comfortable furniture of the drawing room. One huge bookcase was filled with mementos—statues made from wood, metal, marble, and coal, images of the madonna, another of a typical Polish worker, and decorative plates. All were gifts to Lech. Most were given to him by people from the major cities in Poland, others were presented to him during his travels in France, Italy, and Japan. The shelves held an impressive collection of books on European and Polish history, church history, parliamentary procedure for institutions and unions, and a large collection of books on Solidarity printed in Japanese, Finnish, French, German, and Italian.

Now our exchange of family stories began in earnest. The vodka loosened any stiffness our conversation may have had. Always the comedian, my brother Hank, began to put us all at ease. We started to sing, joke, and reflect on our childhood days. We talked about our families, heritage, education, occupations, politics, personal strengths and weaknesses.

Lech challenged Hank on his love for horseradish. Hank met it head-on by eating a heaping teaspoonful, without anything to weaken the taste. Then a jigger of vodka and another teaspoon of horseradish. Lech was wild with laughter.

Others came to the house: Mietek, with his wonderful sense of humor; Maciej, who was eager to hear news about the United States; then another visitor, Lech's family physician, Peter Dyk. The food was passed around again and again. Other friends came and went—names I have forgotten. I was to learn that there was always this constant stream of visitors, punctuated by interruptions from the telephone every half hour or so.

Their questions were endless. What is the price of butter in the United States? How much do shoes, suits, and stockings cost? An automobile? A house? Airfare to Poland?

It also became an intimate evening, filled with emotions. Family and friends looking deeper into each other. Now and then there was a serious comment about the military intervention, the internment, the shortages, and always, concerns for the fate of Solidarity.

Lech and Danuta listen intently to a guest.

Lech's homecoming on November 14, 1982,
eleven months after he was imprisoned
for trying to organize a labor union.

Lech admitted to being forty pounds overweight from the long internment. I wanted to know more about those eleven months. I asked him to recount his daily routine while he was held captive.

"Well, I used to get up at 8 a.m. and say my prayers and have breakfast. At 10 a.m. somebody would bring in all the newspapers. I tried exercising with weights and walking in circles around the room to see if I could lose weight. Sometimes I walked in the garden but I was annoyed by the constant vigilance. I often played table tennis with my guards. We got to know each other on a first name basis. They even asked me for my autograph.

"I would eat lunch about 2 p.m. I used to get soup and a choice of three main courses.

Danuta interrupted, "His favorites were tortellini with cream cheese, and pork and macaroni with jam and cream."

"I would have supper around 7 p.m. and then try to read a lot . . .".

"And, unfortunately, smoke a lot," chimed in Danuta as she went to check on the children.

Lech went on to tell me how he had missed his family and how frustrating it had been not to be able to communicate with them or his friends. He became anxious whenever he heard rumors about the arrest of friends or the harsh political actions that were taking place. And, he longed to attend church.

After a few minutes, Danuta came back into the room, very upset, complaining that the children were behaving badly. They were all in the boys' room having a pillow fight. "They will not stop for me. You're their father, please do something," she said. Lech left us, heading in the direction of the shouting.

The conversation continued in other directions—what kind of clothing people were wearing, how the economies of our two countries were doing. I decided to go back to the bedroom and get my camera. As I walked into the room, I saw five of the children kneeling on the floor, hands folded in prayer, reciting Our Father. Kneeling with them was Lech himself, leading them in their prayer. It was a beautiful scene and I felt uncomfortable invading their privacy, but I was captivated. I delayed leaving, wishing to watch a moment longer. After Our Father, there followed Hail Mary and a prayer for peace for everyone in Poland. Then, standing up, Lech said, "All right everyone, we've said our prayers, the day is over, the fun is over. Now I want you all to go to sleep quietly because your mother is worried about your rest. Into your beds and I'll kiss you good night." I watched a little longer, touched by the peacefulness and calm that filled the room as Lech saw to his family obligations.

Lech's youngest, Wiktoria, shown here a 8½ months, holds a picture of her fathe behind bars.

The christening of Wiktoria. Lech was not present for her birth or baptism because he was being held in prison by the Polish government.

Lech and I returned to the living room. The others began to leave shortly and I could no longer resist the effects of jet lag myself. By 11:00 p.m. the apartment was silent. Our bed was a double convertible sofa located in what served as a study during the day. Hank settled himself on the bed and I lay down myself, shut my eyes, and thought about how beautiful Poland was and how much history there was here. Lech appeared once again in his pajamas, poking his head in our door to say, "Good night, brothers." It certainly was a good night. I wished him well, and was soon asleep.

The next morning, December 7th, the house was already buzzing at seven-thirty. The children were dressing for school. I got dressed, myself, went to the kitchen and watched Danuta start her daily routine. She was preparing breakfast, supervising the children as they dressed and quizzing them about their homework assignments. The four boys—Bogdan (twelve), Slavek (ten), Jarek (nine), and Przemek (seven)—settled down to breakfast.

I watched with delight as they attempted to feign either illness or fullness, rather than finish the meal and be off to school. But they were no match for their mother's stubbornness and discipline. By eight-thirty they were on their way.

I sat and chatted with Danuta while she prepared another round of breakfast. Was she worried over Lech's welfare during his internment? Yes, especially those first three months, not knowing whether Lech was safe or how he was feeling. Their first Christmas separation was unbearable, though many friends came to help. Christmas "Wilija" (pre-Christmas preparation) was sad without him, especially since Danuta was pregnant and needed his support. Dziadek came by every day to offer strength and comfort, and her mother and sister also came as often as possible. Her saddest moments were at night, when the children were all in bed and she was alone without Lech. Wiktoria's birth and christening without him also brought her a great deal of sadness. The length of his internment had frightened her, and she found her first visit during his internment emotionally overwhelming. She visited five times altogether. His homecoming, only two weeks before, now found her and her family caught up again in the full sweep of Lech's activities. At times she regretted that he had not resigned the union leadership when more militant voices prevailed. Lech was an activist, true, but not a militant. Many in the leadership wanted their goals reached more rapidly than he thought possible.

Lech entered the room, already showered and shaved. His simple appearance seemed to energize the whole room. As we sat, Lech asked more questions about his parents' activities during their stay in America and the circumstances concerning their deaths. His mother died in an auto accident in November 1975, and his stepfather suffered a fatal heart attack in August 1981.

Then Lech announced that he was putting his car and driver at our disposal during our stay in Poland. He apologized for not accompanying us on our tour because of restrictions by the government. He was saving his first public appearance since the internment for December 16, 1982, a little more than a week away, at the workers' monument at the Gdansk shipyard gate. He was to make a major address that day, the anniversary of the food riots in December 1970 that left many members dead. The event, its anniversary and the monument that Solidarity had erected there, were all of tremendous spiritual and temperol significance to the entire workers' movement. Lech invited us to return and attend the occasion with him.

I stood up and looked out the window. I was astonished to see lettering on the pavement below: *"Long live Solidarity. We welcome our Lech."* Supporters had painted the greeting for Lech's return from internment two weeks before. I was a little astonished that the authorities would leave that there for so long. Lech shrugged, "Probably because there's a shortage of paint."

Soon after breakfast, Maciej (Lech's aide) arrived and we left with Iza for a more thorough tour of Gdansk. The city has a glitter that instantly appeals to tourists. Once again in the Old Town we visited landmarks where history recorded the Polish spirit: the King Jan Sobieski monument; the King Neptune statue; replicas of centuries-old architecture; the Marjanski Cathedral; St. Brigida's Church (Lech's parish); Oliwa Cathedral (with its famous organ); and Adam Mickiewicz Park with its lake filled with ducks and geese.

We headed for the main post office, an imposing building, which had been reconstructed. A story is told about how two hundred men defended the building against the Nazis for approximately forty days. A steel monument honors their sacrifice. All of the buildings gave some testimony to the destruction inflicted upon this vital seaport during World War II.

I sent some telegrams from this post office to each of the Walesa brothers about their families estate business and requested a family meeting at Iza's home. This done, we returned to Lech's home, hungry and cold, late in the afternoon.

One of Lech's children, Przemek, had developed a fever and Dr. Dyk was summoned. Other guests arrived and left. People asked Lech to attend events

Graffiti written on the street outside Lech's apartment building. It reads "We welcome our Lech."

*The Lady Liberty monument in the Old
Town section of Gdansk, commemorating
200 people who barricaded themselves in
a post office and defended themselves for
45 days against the Nazis.*

The workers' monument that stands at the entrance of the Lenin Shipyard in Gdansk. Lech helped design this memorial to those who died in the 1970 food riots.

Lech goes to confession before a congress session at the first anniversary congress of Solidarity in Gdansk.

Lech speaking at the Warsaw Opera House in October of 1980.

in their community. His leadership role was discussed at length. Other issues were raised as well. Should union membership be maintained? Lech signed autographs and answered questions about his health and morale during internment. Visitors offered to help his family. They always pleaded with him to continue in his leadership role.

After dinner we adjourned to the study and began to distribute the gifts we brought from the United States. The most popular presents were lollipops, soap, and pantyhose. Then we passed around many photographs of the family.

We settled down to more serious talk. I asked Lech how the Polish people were reacting to the government intervention and restrictions, now a year old.

"Whatever happens," he said, "Poland will keep its national identity and pride. Our sense of national pride is a large part of the reason why foreign domination has never succeeded here. There is an obsessive feeling of nationalism born out of repeated challenges. At the center of this unity is the church. It binds us together and makes us one. We have been condemned by either geography or politics, and sometimes both.

"Just look at our history. We've been invaded, partitioned and even wiped off the European political map for one hundred and twenty-three years. But, wartime events and the postwar redrawing of our borders have left Poland more homogeneous than ever before. Ninety-eight percent of our people are still ethnic Poles, and more than ninety percent are Catholic. We are unified, sometimes passively, sometimes actively, but I think we stick together well."

Lech has a way of commanding attention. His oratorical style is arresting—strong, confident, rapid. After a few moments of other chatter I realized how much more I wanted to hear from him. "Now look, don't stop there," I said, somewhat boldly. "There is more than that to your Poland. Please go on."

A puff on a new cigarette seemed to fuel him again. He continued. "Listen to me, my brother. History has been unkind to Poland. Our story is written in blood. Like the trumpeter in Krakow whose song was cut violently when a Tartar's arrow pierced his throat, we continue to remind ourselves of the past to this day. It's a grim reminder of our past and an eerie possibility in the future. And so we are agitated when we recall that one out of every five of our countrymen were killed at the hands of the Nazis. That's six million Polish citizens. Everyone in Poland remembers the past. We will not allow ourselves to repeat it again."

"This is what I think Solidarity helped trigger—a rebirth of Polish national enthusiasm. Our union has been condemned as antisocial, counterrevolutionary, and an agent of Western imperialism. Far more important to us is that it was Polish.

A great Pole, Marshal Joseph Pilsudski has these words on his tomb wall: 'To win and to relax mean disaster; to be defeated and not to surrender, that's victory.' "

I would have liked to hear more, but Hank was already asleep on the couch and Danuta hinted at the time, reminding me of my long ride back to Iza's house the next morning. I would have to wait until another time. But there would be other times. Lech had already made us promise that we would return for his public speech on December 16th, insisting that we accompany him to the monument and stand beside him.

CHAPTER 3
THE BLACK MADONNA

The next morning, Hank, Iza, Bronek, and I left Gdansk in a mild snowstorm. As before, the Skoda was low on oil.

Bronek tried two service stations, without luck. He finally stopped at another station and purchased a quart of oil from a trucker in the area. Not much, but enough to get us back to Sochaczew.

It was a relief to arrive at Iza's house safely. The ride back was longer because of the snow and ice, and somewhat hazardous. But we arrived by six thirty and relaxed for the rest of the night, chatting on till eleven thirty. I distributed more articles of clothing and food to Iza and her family. Then we said good night.

The next morning, we waited for Lech's brothers. Everybody arrived by eleven thirty. I explained their father's estate and affairs. I made the modest distribution involved. Tadeusz, Zygmunt, and Wojtek agreed to go to Warsaw and the American embassy and sign some documents confirming that all the children agreed, as I knew Stanley had wanted, that they would share equally even though only three of them were Stanley's natural children, and the others were their half siblings. We discussed their parents' lives in the Unites States. We drank, joked, and exchanged stories. As usual, Hank delighted everyone with his wit. I felt very comfortable about my administrator's role. All the more so as I saw that things had worked smoothly.

At ten o'clock the next morning, Maciej arrived from Gdansk and announced

The Walesa family:
seated l-r: Edward, Marzena (Iza's daugh-
ter), Iza and Stanley.
standing l-r: Bronek (Iza's husband),
Zygmunt, myself, Tadeusz, Wojciech, and
Marek (Iza's son).

This pin depicting the Black Madonna is worn by Poles to show their allegiance to Solidarity.

he had Lech's car and had been instructed by Lech to give us a tour of Poland. Unbelieveable generosity. Hank and I were elated at this great opportunity to see Poland more closely.

Our first thoughts were to visit another sister of our mother, our Aunt Genowefa, who lives in Plock, a large city of over forty thousand, some fifty miles from Iza. We would bring a bundle of gifts just for her. After that, we planned to see Warsaw and Czestochowa.

The morning was chilly, with some sunshine. At our invitation, Iza came along on our tour. As we started for the main road, I became less concerned with the many anxieties that had preoccupied me earlier. The buildings in the center of Sochaczew were typical of average Polish cities. Not more than three stories high, combining commercial store fronts and private residences above. Most structures were in need of painting. When I pointed this out to Maciej, he assured me it was not from laziness or neglect. There were shortages of all building materials, including paint, and such work had a low priority because of economic conditions in general.

Still, the architecture and street layouts were a pleasure to see. There were many traditional signs, landmarks of the old Poland: immense churches with towering arches, small shrines to the Holy Mother along the roadside, public buildings where town fathers conducted community affairs.

Many of the newer homes were sparely constructed with oversized cinder and cement blocks, and usually left unpainted. Outside almost every city there were usually fields and forests. The white birch trees were unbelievably lovely. Each mile of country was more breathtaking than the last. The roads were lined with handsome and majestic trees. The air seemed clean and healthy. As always, the ever-present crows dotted the countryside.

I had grown to feel safe in Poland. The military presence was not always obvious. And it seemed that Poland was unchanged despite the military intervention.

The next day, we journeyed to Czestochowa, starting on a cold morning with the smell of snow in the air. We said good-bye to our aunt. The parting was naturally emotional. We left as much as we could of ourselves, material and financial. It was a good way to cement our ties after such a short time.

We were glad Maciej was along. He was an ideal companion for tourists like ourselves. Having graduated from Warsaw University with a major in accounting and economics, his knowledge of the history, background, and culture of his country satisfied our constant curiosity, especially our many questions about social and economic conditions since the end of World War II. Over the next three days, we were able to get from Maciej an education and a glimpse into the heart of many events that to us had only been superficial reporting.

Our first stop along the way was at Frederic Chopin's birthplace in Zelozowa Wola. The building was small but well appointed, with enough room for a housekeeper and servant. A large oak tree in front of the house added to the peaceful setting.

Chopin's home had been a pleasant and comfortable one. There was a lot of natural light in the rooms, all of which were convenient to the kitchen, the traditional source of warmth and center of much family activity. Chopin's bedroom is now empty except for a large vase filled with fresh flowers. All of the furniture that had once belonged to the young genius has been lost to private collectors. But the beauty and simplicity of the large floral arrangement was enough. We toured the grounds and visited the gravesite and took pictures. Later we were to find many more indications of Chopin's effect on Poland. It was as if each section of the country had adopted the gifted young composer for its own. He slept here, concertized there, visited at another, lunched somewhere else; each place with a plaque proudly proclaiming the connection. It did not surprise me, for I had long ago fallen under the spell of his polonaises, mazurkas, and ballades.

Warsaw was our next stop. Maciej took us to a restaurant in the Old Town for venison steak. We relaxed in the pleasant atmosphere. Hank and I enjoyed wine and beer, but not so Maciej. The law against drunk driving is very strict in Poland. In fact, anyone who takes a sip of alcohol and drives might be arrested. Maciej rushed us so that we could get started for Czestochowa and witness the closing of the shrine of the Black Madonna. In ten minutes we were on the highway.

We had to stop for gas. Maciej found a station about ten minutes out of Warsaw. While the attendant was refueling the car Maciej pulled out his ration coupons and registration for identification. Once the attendant realized that the car, a Polenez, belonged to Lech Walesa, he became excited and called his partner over. For a minute I thought a serious problem was developing, but that was not the case. After a small conference they returned to Maciej and asked if he would mind allowing them to pay for the gas. Maciej was slightly embarrassed and taken by surprise, but they told him that it was a small gesture

The mile-long cross of flowers near the Shrine of the Black Madonna at Czesto- chowa.

on their part to show their loyalty and support for Lech. Maciej consented. Both attendants gave our Polenez a quick check under the hood, and as we were pulling away, they flashed the now familiar "V" sign for hope and victory.

On the road once again, Maciej was the first to speak. "That, my friends, is one of the many expressions of the spirit of Solidarity."

About a half hour into the journey I became curious about the lack of roadside directions to Czestochowa, the most popular shrine in Poland, hosting well over a million pilgrims a year. It was strange that for a city of such worldwide repute there were no road signs. I asked Maciej about this. "Perhaps it is a government oversight," he smiled, but then added, "from which our Holy Mother has not suffered."

It was dark when we pulled into the courtyard of the Paulist Monastery at the Church of Jasna Gora in Czestochowa. We felt strange parked alone in the middle of this large place, almost as though we had committed a traffic violation and were now detained. Maciej assured us that we would be regarded as guests of Lech, and that the hospitality of the monastery would soon be evident.

Maciej disappeared into the building and left us in the courtyard. We got out, stretched our legs and began to look at the history around us. High walls of stone and concrete surrounded the cobblestoned courtyard that was neat and well kept. The buttressed walls hinted at the enormous weight they supported. Built like a fortress six hundred years ago to protect the inhabitants from invaders and bandits, it was here that the Sacred portrait of Our Lady of Czestochowa, the famous Black Madonna, was kept.

After about fifteen minutes, Maciej reappeared with Father Ireneus Pompa, one of the eighty-nine priests who care for the shrine of the Madonna. Hank and I were introduced as the cousins of Lech Walesa from the United States. Father Pompa was all excitement and courtesy, expressing his deep satisfaction at extending the hospitality of the Paulist fathers. We were honored and privileged ourselves.

We were led to quarters reserved for visiting clergy and dignitaries where women were not allowed. The entrance was, in fact, guarded by an elderly nun. We were told that when Lech visits Czestochowa, Danuta is directed to other quarters for overnight stays. An exception to this rule is made only for kings and queens from other countries. Maciej told me that the first time the Walesas came here, Danuta, always close to Lech, was startled when someone's hands on her shoulders held her back before she could step into the "forbidden" zone reserved for men only. She let out a yell that probably reached the farthest

A wooden relief of the Black Madonna.

Lech and Danuta attend Mass at the Shrine of the Black Madonna.

Lech and Danuta receive Communion at the Shrine.

corners of the monastery. The person restraining Danuta was this same nun we had just seen. Startled by such an outcry, the nun had gripped Danuta even tighter. It took Lech and the others a minute or so to quiet both women and return things to the calm, peacefulness of this holy place.

Maciej and Father Pompa reminded us we had only three or four minutes to witness the closing of the Madonna's portrait. The portrait is displayed daily between the hours of 6 a.m. and 8:30 p.m., after which a panel covers the sacred icon to preserve the centuries-old pigmentation.

We raced through darkened hallways and stairways, scarcely noting the many historical pieces on the walls and pedestals. Then we were led to a door which opened to a marble balustrade at the side of the altar of the Madonna. A novena had just finished and everyone began to kneel for the closing.

I could feel the history of the place. A nervous excitement filled me as I knelt twenty feet from the Madonna. She was elevated about ten feet above the altar. From the corner of my eye I was able to see hundreds of heads straining behind the wooden gates. I felt like a bandit, thinking I did not deserve this special privilege of being so close.

I remembered how Lech had apologized for not being able to accompany us. "But," he said, "the people you meet know this and they will understand. My spirit will always be with you wherever you go. You can play a fortunate and timely role for me and for them. Through you and Henry, the people will see how the spirit of Solidarity still touches me, and how it will revive them and they will revive me also."

I was jolted from these thoughts by the blare of a trumpet and the thump of a timpani as the closing ceremony began. As the instruments played out their fanfare, a gold-and-silver inlaid panel began to rise slowly from the bottom of the picture. I was annoyed at whatever had kept us from getting here sooner, because now that I had my chance to study the Holy Mother, patron saint of Poland, she was being stored away for the night. I began to say Hail Mary prayers and to study the gem encrusted Madonna. I don't know if I ever finished the prayer because my eyes darted from one detail to another. The dress of the Madonna was incredibly ornate. Here a cross or a crown, there an initial or floral pattern finely etched and holding a variety of precious stones. I focused my eyes on the necklace, an unusual arrangement made entirely of gold rings. As I gazed at these rings I thought of the story behind them. They were the actual wedding bands of many married couples in the seventeenth century who wished to express their faith in the Holy Mother. I tried to absorb as much as I could before the panel covered Our Lady's face. There were indeed the dark slashes on the cheek, said to be from the sword of an infidel invader. Six hundred years of survival. Amazing. Before I could study the crown, the panel was completely closed and the ceremony over. It was truly breathtaking. So many years of reverence from kings, queens, generals, and statesmen who had come here to pay homage to the miracles of this Madonna. Even Poles in the United States have never lost this faith. In Doylestown, Pennsylvania there is a replica of the Madonna, visited by thousands of Americans each year.

With the closing, people began to file out of the church. I caught Father Pompa's eye, and he motioned me to follow him. Henry and I followed him back through the shadows again only to emerge in the courtyard where we had parked our car.

Father Pompa was anxious to welcome us more formally and apologized for the hasty pace we had been put through since our arrival. He made it very clear that the Monastery of Jasna Gora ("Bright Mountain" in English) would be our home until we left the area. We toured the courtyards and the perimeter of the church grounds, and learned that the church really was built like a fortress. Centuries ago marauding bandits had always come here, hoping to steal the treasure that had accumulated from many years of devotion by various kingdoms and noblemen.

We began Sunday by attending mass at the chapel and witnessing the opening of the Madonna. We sat in the section for regular church members and attended the mass as they would.

Once again the drum roll began, announcing the uncovering of the Madonna. Trumpets blared and the wooden panel began to move down and expose the sacred Mother of God. All eyes were fixed on one spot. I noticed a woman in tears with hands folded in prayer, a man looking up with hope in his face, another looking longingly with lips moving in prayer, another swaying slightly. One man particularly caught my attention. He was about seventy-five or eighty years old, white-haired with a white walrus-like mustache. His hands moved together as tears rolled down his leathered face. I prayed that his wishes and hopes would be answered, whatever they were.

It was difficult to concentrate on the Mass with so many strange sights before me. I looked at the walls of the chapel intently, and Maciej noticed my curiosity. "Take special note on what you see," he said. "There on the walls are the hopes and prayers of many worshippers. There are the pins, brooches, crosses, and medals of thousands who have visited here. You'll notice among them many Solidarity pins from different factories throughout Poland. Make note of those two braces and those crutches, which signify that some sort of miracle has been attributed to our Holy Mother. They say that our Black Madonna is responsible for a bona fide miracle at least once every hundred years."

"One more thing," he added, "those pins and other objects were put there by the person himself. The church's help is not requested. Individuals come in with stools and ladders, and even climb on someone else's back to affix their offerings.

The wall was also a treasure of sorts, for I could see gold, silver and other precious metals hanging there. "People," Maciej added, "bring valuable jewelry in hopes that the Paulist fathers might use them for their next dress on the Madonna."

My eyes next turned to the altar. Whatever silver or gold graced the altar, was framed by dark, almost black, walls or columns. Sheepishly, I asked Maciej why the altar was painted black. Maciej quickly clarified: "It's not painted, it's natural. The dark is the natural color of ebony wood, a very rare gift from nature. Almost as valuable as gold."

The Mass was over and the worshippers began to empty out of the chapel. We began to tour other sections of the church when Father Pompa caught up with us, and we saw in the daylight what we could not appreciate the night before.

As we turned back to the rooms inside the church, we came upon another Paulist priest. Father Pompa introduced us to Father Szymon (Simon) Stefanowicz, a senior resident at the monastery. Father Stefanowicz had just returned from an eight-year tour of the United States. His home for the last three years had been Saint Ambrose's Church in Old Bridge, New Jersey, the very same church of which my brother Henry was a member. It was unbelievable. Henry had known that a priest from Poland was visiting his church but had never met him. It boosted our spirits to speak with someone whose English was so good. Together, we all headed to the "treasure room".

The list of treasures located there could go on for several pages. But our biggest surprise came when we viewed an oil-on-canvas portrait of what appeared to be Lech Walesa. What was it doing here? Father Simon saw our surprise and said with a wry smile, "Clever, isn't it? But, you know, it's more than that. This painting was done by an unknown artist who attempted to depict

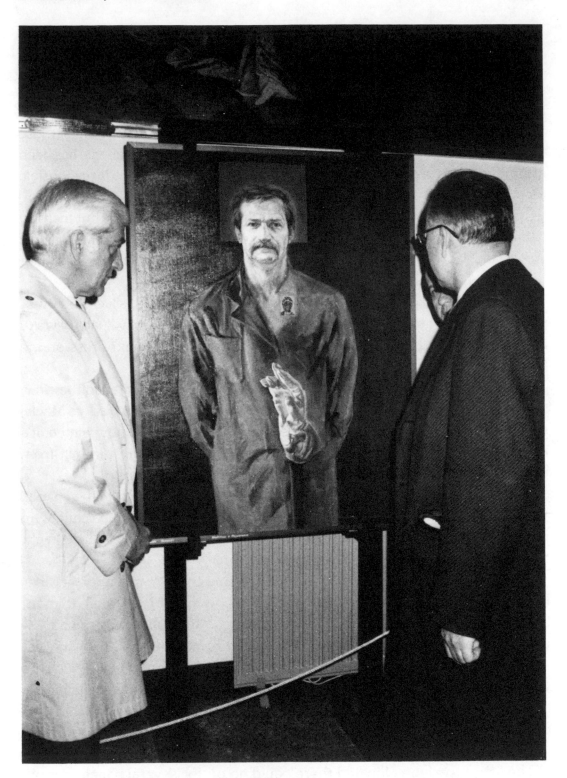

This portrait of a typical Polish worker hangs in the Treasury Room of the Black Madonna. The amazing resemblance to Lech remains unexplained, since it was painted four years before he became a union activist and he never posed for the portrait.

a typical Polish working man. It was done at least four years before Lech joined any union organization. It was brought to us in 1980 by a priest who thought the resemblance was remarkable, possibly a miracle, or a smile from the Madonna. We had already asked Lech about it, but he swears he never posed for any portrait for anyone." I took a photograph of it because I knew people would want to see this in the United States.

Next we went through the arsenal room. Here there were muskets, spears, lances, swords, knives, and other weapons. Some were rich in royal Polish designs, others had been captured in prior wars.

Our tour of these rooms came to an end when Father Simon announced that it was time for lunch. "Good heavens, it's late. You must be starved. What would Lech think of me? We're going to the refectory."

What he called a refectory was now a dining room. It was a large, beautiful room, with a ceiling painted in rich colors depicting religious events. A room fit for kings. We were told that the architecture and paintings dated back to 1670.

There were about two hundred people eating there at the moment. Most of them were visiting priests. Henry took this opportunity to indulge in some New Jersey and St. Ambrose's Church nostalgia with Father Simon. We spent an hour in that room exchanging stories and jokes, and Father Simon introduced us to many interested onlookers who had detected our American English. There were questions about our politics, schools, automobiles, and the jeans craze. Father Simon interrupted once again to bring our tour to an end before we had to depart. It was with reluctance that we said our goodbyes, but Father Simon was determined to show us more of the monastery.

We passed through halls, exploring chambers and rooms that were not often used. Many of the treasures we saw during our walk were unlit and hidden from public view. If it were not for my pocket flashlight I could not have appreciated them. There were portraits of kings, dukes, and lords; of bishops, cardinals, and popes; and pictures of events in the distant past. I think I counted eight different portraits of our Polish Pope, all waiting for some other time and place for public display.

We were shown the room where people of special distinction would be quartered for the night—where Cardinal Wyszinski or Cardinal Glemp would stay and where Pope John Paul slept during visits to Czestochowa. Quiet, secluded and comfortable, it gave easy access to all points in the church. Above all, it seemed that the room was located in the most isolated section of the monastery to protect important visitors from intruders. Father Simon insisted that he had something better to show us. We came to an archway over a stairway, studded with delicately inlaid wood designs, which ended at a double door that was also etched with fine inlaid woods. As senior resident and caretaker of the church records, Father Simon had the key to this room. He opened the door, revealing a huge room filled with large volumes of books from floor to ceiling.

"Gentlemen," Father Simon announced, "our biblioteque room, or library, as you might call it. This room contains the history of the church at Czestochowa. This is where our Pope John Paul met with all the church officials in Poland when he first visited us. In this private room he was able to communicate to us the future of the church in Poland. Two hundred and twenty-five members were addressed by the Pope in this room. Here is where the Pope sat. Please note the beautiful wood carving of this chair, which bears the coat of arms of the Paulist order. You may touch and examine the chair, but please do not sit in it."

"The two tables in this room were specially made inside this room. They cannot be removed from this room because they will not fit through that doorway. The inlay on each is made of the finest woods selected for the beauty of their grains. The books ringing this room were all handcrafted. The calligraphy and plates inside these pages were made by hand, by talented Paulist fathers. Each book is an original and the only one of its kind. Let me show you."

He took down two books and placed them on a table. He flicked through the pages and opened to one very colorful page. I could not believe my eyes. I had often seen pictures of plates like this in my *National Geographic,* but not the real thing. I came very close in order to look at the details. Father Simon sensed my curiosity and appreciation and said, "Go ahead, touch it, but gently. I can see it means a great deal to you."

He then picked up the book and showed us the date when it was written: 1724. Then he told me to hold open my arms and feel the weight of the book. It was heavy. "Notice the binding and sewing, all handmade," he said.

He put the books away and led us to a table where he took down two more books. "This," he said, "is the visitors registry book. When a famous guest visits us, we take him here to the bibliotheque room and have him sign the guest book. Look, here is your President John F. Kennedy's signature. And here, the King of Norway. And here, your cousin Lech Walesa." He opened another guest book. Then, before showing us the book, he told us this story.

"During World War II when the Nazis occupied Poland, Adolf Hitler designated General Frank as Primate of the Church of Poland. This is the elected position by the church now held by Cardinal Glemp and, before him, by Cardinal Wyszinski. The Primate's office was a very responsible position in the old days. When a king left our country to fight a war somewhere or to visit another country, he delegated all his administrative powers to the Primate.

"Hitler knew the power of that office; therefore he posted one of his generals in that position to control the church. And so it was in 1940 that General Frank came with his wife to Czestochowa. When he came into this room to sign the register he was refused. He insisted, as Primate, that he had the right, and no one could stop him. He came with troops and guns. Reluctantly, the guest book was opened to him, but somehow the pen did not work. Repeated attempts at the inkwell failed. He shook the pen. A small blot of ink fell on the page and he was finally able to sign his name. After he left, however, the blot spread over his name and it has remained that way to this day. Now look at his signature and see how divine providence resisted also."

I looked with Henry and we were amazed. Sure enough, a large portion of his name was blotted out. "Would you call it another miracle of our wonderful Madonna?" Father Simon asked. "And now, my brothers from America, please sit, for I would like you to sign the register as cousins of Lech Walesa from the United States."

As Henry and I both signed, we felt Lech's presence more than ever. Lech was right about the people. Through us they related to Lech.

"And now, my dear friends, I have two more privileges left for you before you leave. We will go to the souvenir shop where I will ask my brothers to open their store just for you. Normally we do not open the shop on Sundays. But this is a special occasion."

Once in the shop, Henry and I lost ourselves, as any tourist would. In half an hour, our arms were loaded with bundles. "All right, come with me," Father Simon insisted. "We will all go to the sacristy, where I will give you one of my 'wholesale' blessings on all your religious articles."

"As a final privilege, from me to you, I want to take you back to the altar of our Madonnna for the day's closing, which is early today because there is no service this evening." Once again, we walked briskly through the halls to reach the Madonna's chapel. Going from one level to another, around corners and through doors, I lost my sense of direction. Then suddenly we stood before a

I sign the guest book at the library in the Shrine while my brother Hank, Father Simon and Father Pompa look on.

door and were instructed to be absolutely quiet when we entered because of the religious service that was in progress.

Henry and I were totally unprepared for what we were about to experience. In an instant the door was opened and Father Simon motioned us to follow and stand beside a priest who was kneeling at the steps before an altar. The priest was concluding the final passages of Hail Mary, then, catching sight of us, he moved over a bit so that we could kneel beside him. He was praying to the Holy Madonna. The sacred painting was barely six or seven feet from us. Behind him the chapel was crowded with people. We were standing at the very foot of the altar, then both of us quickly dropped to our knees, feeling awkward about blocking someone else's view.

Looking up from this position, the Polish Madonna was almost within our reach. My eyes focused on all the details of the bejeweled Holy Mother. Suddenly, the trumpets sounded and the timpani announced a closing once more. My eyes became moist. It was a deeply religious experience for both of us.

It was over. Father Simon came over to us and said, "Come here, my brothers. Touch the altar, touch the candlesticks. Look into her eyes. She follows you wherever you stand. Tell everyone what you felt and saw here. Tell all Americans about the charisma of our Polish Madonna."

We moved away from the altar and into the outer chambers, exchanging our feelings about the experience. Father Simon added, "And now come to my chambers and share my coffee or tea and we will toast Lech."

Another half hour of thoughts about America, Poland, the people and Lech. We shared deep feelings about our roots and the future, about the heyday of Solidarity, about the nation's rebirth, and about continuing American support.

But the time finally came for goodbyes. Father Simon gave us some written messages for friends in New Jersey. The last twenty-four hours were a high spot for both of us and it seemed that way for our two hosts as well. The traditional hug and cheek kiss cemented our ties. We headed for Sochaczew to Iza's house and some rest.

CHAPTER 4
THE LONG JOURNEY TO GDANSK

We stayed at Iza's until December 15, 1982, when we repacked our belongings and headed for Lech's for our last two days in Poland. It was noon when we climbed into a taxi for Warsaw, the first stop on our way.

We had arranged to meet a newspaper editor of a popular Warsaw daily in the Hotel Forum lobby. The lobby was crowded. A woman approached us for an exchange of some dollars and Hank became nervous. He wondered if we were being set up. The sensitivity of our position made us both very cautious. We felt as though many eyes were on us. I myself thought I caught one stranger's stare several times.

The editor finally arrived and attempted to help us arrange a flight from Warsaw to Gdansk. We were told that the flight was booked solid and that all flights were grounded because of bad weather in Gdansk. We were advised by the hotel that if we went to the airport we might be able to board if there were cancellations. Someone who had overheard our conversation, and that we were going to see Lech, handed us a note informing us that we were being watched and should exercise caution.

The next series of events were quite an experience for us. After waiting forty-five minutes at the terminal we decided to go by train. Just as we emerged

Walter Cronkite greets Lech in Warsaw before doing an interview with him for CBS.

Lech meets with Father Jankowski in front of St. Brigitte's Church in Gdansk.

October 14, 1981. Lech holds a press conference, and is asked about the threat of the Soviet Union. He responds, "The Soviet Union says it is Poland's friend, and there is surely no need to fear one's friend."

In his first "crowd" appearance since martial law was declared a year earlier, Lech and Danuta attend a requiem Mass for Walesa's close friend and counselor, Bishop Kazimierz Kluz, 25, who died in an automobile accident.

November 17, 1982. Walesa, Danuta, and Father Jankowski go to see Archbishop Kaczmarek in Gdansk.

Lech and Polish primate Jozef Glemp after one of their many lengthy talks to discuss the Church's delicate role in the Solidarity movement.

1980. Walesa is cheered by crowds in Cracow as he pledges to continue efforts to gain final official approval for Solidarity.

1981. Lech takes time off from his endless rounds of meetings to do some sightseeing in Paris.

from the terminal a man approached us and offered to take us to Gdansk in his taxi. Hours ago he had driven someone to Warsaw and wanted to return to Gdansk with another fare. We agreed to hire his cab, got in and drove only a hundred feet when we were stopped by airport police.

The driver was asked to accompany two officials for a private conference. We had waited in the cab for an anxious fifteen minutes, when our driver returned and told us that he could not take us to Gdansk because his out-of-town solicitation for fares was illegal at the airport. We removed our baggage, distressed at the prospect of a long train ride. Just before we parted, the cab driver whispered that he would meet us at the train station and take us to our destination. At the Warsaw train station, I felt as if I was acting a part in a movie script. There we were in the midst of another crowded public space, looking for a man who was a stranger to both of us. Just as we were about to give up, the taxi driver appeared. We got into the taxi quickly and slammed the doors. The driver blessed himself, and we headed north for Gdansk, 220 miles away.

After about fifteen minutes, the driver started to talk to us. His name was Jan. He was married, with two children, and had been hacking fares for about seven years. When he found out we were going to Lech's house and who we were, he became very interested in our American attitudes towards the troubles in Poland. There was much exchange of information between us and I knew the five hour ride would seem much shorter. How wrong I was!

We started at 2 p.m. The weather was turning colder. At five o'clock, the sky was very dark and it started to snow. We were forced to reduce our speed to about thirty-five miles an hour. Seeing ahead was difficult. The road was dark and becoming treacherous. We were all looking ahead, and Hank and I wondered if we should stop until it was over. "Don't worry, Mr. Henry," Jan assured us. "No problem."

About seven o'clock, Hank asked why the yellow light on the dash was blinking. "It's a warning that the fuel tank is low," Jan said. "But don't worry, no problem, there's a gas station up ahead."

About a half hour later, we pulled into a pitch black driveway. Jan said, "Well, this is the gas station."

"But it's dark and it seems deserted," I said.

"Don't worry, Mr. Walter, there's someone in there. I'll be right back." The whole atmosphere was unbelievable. I began to pick out several other cars parked there too. I was barely able to follow the dark shadow of Jan, when I noticed a tiny glow from a candle appear from inside the building. My hopes of getting to Lech's house at a reasonable hour seemed dashed for the moment. After a long five minutes Jan gave us the sad news: "They had a blackout in this region because of the storm, and the electric pumps for the gas tanks are not working. We can't get any gas until the electricity is restored. But don't worry, no problem. The service will be restored very soon."

I wondered at his words. After a half hour, I asked Jan if he had enough gas to reach the next gas station. Jan felt that he did, if he detoured through Elblag, ten or twelve miles away. And so, with another assurance from Jan, "Don't worry, no problem we can make it", we took off into the dark night, yellow light blinking and fingers crossed.

After fifteen minutes the car sputtered to a halt, out of gas. By now the snow had stopped. The sky was clear and we wondered what to do next. Jan, undaunted, gave further assurance that we would get help from a passing motorist. By now, Hank was working on his third pack of cigarettes for the day. We were both upset over the prospect of spending the night in the car.

A half hour passed. Someone stopped and pulled up in front of our car and attached a cable to our bumper. In a few minutes we were on our way with a tow from a small bus heading for Gdansk. Jan said confidently, "I told you we had no problem. He'll pull us into the next station on his way to Gdansk. So sit back and relax."

About fifteen minutes later, our hopes were dashed again. The tow cable snapped. As Jan got out of the cab, I swear I could hear him say, "Don't worry about a thing." The cable was difficult to repair. It could not handle the load. Hank wondered if some fuel might have shifted around and would give us a start. It was worth a try. Jan quickly got in, confident that the cab was going to make it. It started. We waved our thanks to the driver who had given us the tow and headed straight for the station at Elblag. We arrived and were able to get a full tank. "I told you, we had no problem," Jan said triumphantly.

We were on the last leg of our journey and the snowfall was now very light. As we approached Gdansk the road was clean and the streets were quiet. We drove into the center of that beautiful city. All the buildings took on a special charm in the subdued light of the street lamps. The peeling and fading paint was not so noticeable. The lights in the windows of the buildings looked friendly. Just as I was lost in a reverie, two uniformed militiamen turned the corner, their superior officer in the lead. They were marching stiffly and appeared to be making a tour of duty.

It occured to me that this was the night before Lech was to make his first public appearance since his internment. We had just passed the monument where Lech was to speak in a few hours. In the darkness the three crosses commemorating the men who had died twelve years before were just barely visible. I could picture the multitude standing there tomorrow. It was rumored that forty thousand people would attend.

Lech had told us that his first words to the public would be reassuring: that his internment had not changed his views about keeping alive an independent workers' union, that his first objective would be to demand that the military release all those still interned, and that he be allowed to resume his leadership role for a workers' voice within the government.

It was 11 p.m. when we turned into the Street of Pilots. I was concerned about ringing Lech's bell at this hour of the night. Danuta would be frightened about Lech's welfare, and Lech would likely be anxious also. Even though he had made two formal requests to the authorities to be allowed to speak publicly on December 16, he never received official acknowledgment or approval from them.

In the dark, all the doorways to this huge apartment complex looked alike, so it was difficult to be sure which was Lech's section. After trying one entrance and not finding his nameplate, I proceeded to the next, while Hank waited for me in the cab.

As I walked the short distance, I noticed eight or nine people across the street looking through their car windows at me. My guard was up and I felt somewhat tense, but I proceeded as calmly as possible, trying not to notice the men who were getting out of the cars. I reached the inside of the lobby, feeling slightly relieved, and started for the steps. The hall was so dimly lit that I almost fell over two men who were sitting at the foot of the stairway. They were as startled as I was. As I apologized for the interruption, I saw that they were wearing uniforms. One had a pistol, and the other a rifle over his right shoulder. My adrenalin shot up slightly. We confronted each other, speechless for a moment. I was the first to speak, if only to conceal my jitters. "Is there something wrong here? Isn't this the building where Lech Walesa lives?"

For a few seconds they seemed to be caught off guard. I must have looked like an official, dressed in my dark business suit and tie. I got the impression they were paying me the kind of respect they would normally reserve for a superior officer. For a moment I felt in control of the situation. They responded, almost meekly, that Lech did live here. They then asked me respectfully but firmly who I was. I explained the situation and that Lech was expecting me. They asked me to wait, while one of them went to get the officer in charge. In an instant a man in civilian clothes appeared and asked for my papers. I repeated my story and was told to wait while he checked my papers with someone outside. As my passport and visa disappeared with this stranger, I experienced a helplessness of being without identification in a foreign country.

As I waited, I noticed a third person, also in a military uniform, sitting above us on the steps leading to the next floor. It occurred to me that I had left Hank waiting in the cab. He must have become anxious about the presence of so many people darting in and out of the building I had gone into. I decided to reassure him, so I informed the guards that I would return very shortly while I went to get my brother. I had taken only one step when I felt the pressure of a hand on my right arm and a voice asking me to please wait. I waited two more minutes, certain that Hank must have exhausted all his cigarettes by this time. I turned to the young militiaman, my hand now holding his arm, and said, "Look, I've got a brother in the taxi waiting for me, probably frightened by all the activity going on here. You have my passport and other ID, so I'm not going anywhere without them." I took two more steps down, not quite sure of myself, and turned again to him, "Now, you just wait here and I'll call my brother."

I felt brave as I walked out. I told Hank the story and brought him back with me to the tiny cramped hallway. There were now about a dozen men standing in front of the building. More minutes passed. Hank and I went back inside and attempted to socialize with the militia.

Finally, our papers came back with the senior officer, who apologized for the delay. The tension in the atmosphere quickly disappeared. His curiosity about our stay in Poland, which state we were from, and our relationship to the Walesas, appeared to be genuine. My engineering background, documented on the visa, invited various questions also. At last, he wished us a pleasant night and a good stay in Poland, and very politely, escorted us closer to Lech's doorway.

It was eleven-forty. I rang the bell nervously. Dziadek's large frame appeared in the open doorway. He recognized us and quickly let us in. We talked in whispers and asked if we could spend the night without disturbing anyone else. But in two minutes, Danuta's sleepy eyes met our exhausted stares and she ushered us to the same room we had occupied a week before. Our eyes were shut by twelve thirty.

CHAPTER 5
LECH GOES FOR A RIDE

At eight the next morning, a voice shouted at us, "Wake up, wake up, sleepy ones. Breakfast is ready. No time to rest. We have to prepare for the big moment today." It was Lech, standing in the doorway. He came into the center of the room laughing and, said, "How did you like your reception committee? Come, get up and tell me about your interesting evening." We chatted a bit and he left us to shower, shave, and dress. As soon as I was ready, I made my way to the busy kitchen. The two oldest children were finishing their eggs and milk. Danuta was asking each one about his homework. Her questioning was pointed and direct. She seemed to know already whose work was less than complete. She was right. Przemek, was trying to avoid looking at her or answering her questions, pretending to have an intense interest in his food.

"Przemek, you're an actor. You and I know you hate those eggs. Answer your mother," Lech said.

"No, no, Dad, they really are exceptional today."

"Aren't you the foxy one," Lech quipped, a thin smile on his face. Lech looked at Danuta, who was getting impatient. She then took Przemek by the arm and marched him to his bedroom. I could hear the child's excuses.

Hank came into the kitchen just as Danuta was taking Przemek back to his room. "What's going on?" he asked.

"I have a delinquent son who must be dealt with later," Lech said. "You see, my brothers, I have sometimes been less than attentive to my children. It has been difficult for me and for them. Eleven months of internment have not helped either. God only knows how much of a burden that woman has had to carry. My work is a curse on them. The children have had many pressures from other children, as well as from the school. I shall have to resume my father's role more responsibly. Thank God for Danuta, thank God for my aides and friends who have tried to help."

Danuta came back to the kitchen to make sure our breakfast was in progress and then returned to the hallway, where the children were about to leave for school. I could hear some last minute instructions and admonitions for better work that day. Back in the kitchen, she faced Lech, pointing at him with a spoon in her hand, and said, "Lech, you are going to have to do something about that boy tonight. He needs to feel your presence. You must demand more from him. He's not listening to me. I've warned you about him before."

Lech could respond only by pointing out what we already knew.

"You know what it's been like this past week. I promise I'll talk to him after school, *if I'm here.*"

I began to eat, trying to avoid any more of an intrusion into their affairs.

"Now, tell me," Lech said, "what happened to you last night?" We told him about our trip back in the storm, the cab driver, the snapped cable, everything. There was laughter at the driver's "Don't worry about a thing." Lech told us that a group of men now outside his apartment were TV media people. He had just learned that their papers had been confiscated at 2 a.m. last night and they had been told to go to the Gdansk police station to reclaim them. (The papers were not returned until 2 p.m. that afternoon.)

When we had finished breakfast, Lech motioned us to come to the study. He took us to the window and pointed, "Can you see anything different about the activity out there today, my brothers?"

Looking out the window, which was at the back of the house, I began to study for the first time the rear of the property. The large apartment buildings, housing about thirty families each, were set in a crescent shape surrounding a recreational garden that was still under development. A lonely passerby looked up at our window and smiled at us. Lech waved in recognition. Two roads led into this building complex. Lech caught our confused expressions and explained: "Look at the end of the road. See the military truck and car and two

Lech's look-alike brother Stanley.

or three militiamen standing guard? They are checking everyone going out and coming in. Don't you get it? Know what's happening? They will not allow anyone in to see me. Haven't you noticed that Mietek and Maciej are not here yet? It's past nine. They usually get here by eight-thirty. The bad guys and the good guys are playing their games again today. They are going to make it difficult for me to get to the monument. Well, this is not going to intimidate me. I'm still going. If you're not frightened by this, I would like you to join me. Are you willing?"

Before either of us could answer, the doorbell rang. It was Stanley Walesa, Lech's look-alike brother. "How did you get here?" Lech asked.

"They tried to stop me, but I persisted," Stanley replied.

We had no sooner sat down for another cup of tea when the doorbell rang again. Dziadek looked through the peephole and said he did not recognize the visitor and that he did not look like one of "them". "Well, if he got this far," Lech said, "find out who he is." The door was opened slightly and the visitor announced that he was from a section of Poland miles away and wanted to see Lech about a union matter and join him at the monument when he spoke there.

"Let him in," shouted Lech.

The new guest was Zbygniew. He had been traveling for ten hours by train, all night. Lech greeted him and Danuta made a sandwich for him and a cup of tea. He told us his story. The people in his community were anxious to resume a dialogue with the government, and would Lech please advise them of the best course to follow? Would Lech support a letter to Chairman Jaruzelski which they had drafted?

Lech was touched by the action and the interest their letter showed. It reaffirmed their confidence in Lech as the man to represent them. If Mr. Walesa felt the timing of the letter was incorrect, they would be guided by his judgment and wait for another opportunity.

In the meantime there were many attempts to reach Mietek and Maciej by phone. Their phones were "out of order." I decided this was a good time to take some pictures of Lech and his family.

Hank looked out the kitchen window at the front of the building and confirmed that the militia guards were on that side of the property also. We began to pick them out, altogether about eight or ten at various access points to the apartment complex. Danuta commented on the reports we had that there were already about eight thousand people at the monument. It was to be a thrilling and emotional event. Lech himself was already caught up in events planned for that day, and was inspired by the projected turnout.

I returned to the study just as Zbygniew and Stanley were leaving Lech to get another cup of tea in the kitchen. I faced Lech with my camera and asked if he could pose for me at the window. I sensed his annoyance at the request.

"I'm not an actor," he said. "I don't know how to pose for anything. You'll have to take your shots as you see them."

I felt selfish and sorry. He must have felt many anxieties at this moment. I asked him if he thought that there would be many people at the monument and whether our presence there might make things more uncomfortable for him than he thought. Before he could answer, the doorbell rang. Dziadek went to the peephole and hurried back to Lech. "They're here," he said, "The militia."

"Find out what they want," said Lech.

As soon as Dziadek had unlatched the door and turned the knob, pressure from the other side pushed it open wide. Six men in uniform entered the room, walked over to Lech and formed a circle around him. Four of them had rifles, slung on their shoulders, and two wore holstered pistols, their hands resting on their weapons. They opened their tight circle wide enough for one more person to join them, apparently their superior officer.

"Mr. Walesa," said their leader, "please get your hat and coat and come with us."

"Where am I going?" Lech asked.

"Mr. Walesa," the leader replied, "we do not wish any trouble. Please get your hat and coat and come with us."

Once more Lech said, "I don't intend to trouble you or anyone else. Just tell me where we are going."

The officer, now obviously annoyed, said, "Mr. Walesa, you have been asked to report to the office of the Minister of Finance twice before. Since you have disregarded both these requests, we have been instructed to take you there."

By this time, the doorbell and the activity in the hall and study attracted Danuta's attention. She quickly came into the room, demanding, "What are you people doing here? Lech, what is going on? Honey, please tell me." Lech's response was interrupted by Danuta's voice once more, now more emotional: "I don't believe it. What has this man done to you?" She moved in among them, breaking the tight circle and placing herself in the center with Lech.

"Tell me, I demand that you tell me," she shouted, "what has this man done that you come in here like this? Haven't you held him long enough? He's the father of seven children, he's my husband, he's been with you for eleven months."

The air became charged. Everyone was nervous, including myself. I was six feet from the group, with a camera in my hand. One of the soldiers carrying a rifle looked at me and the camera. Slowly I placed the camera on the windowsill beside me and folded my arms in front of me.

Danuta's accusations towards the visitors were becoming more personal and abrasive. It appeared that no one knew how to handle Danuta's intervention. Then Lech, who was the calmest, pleaded, "Honey, please calm down, these *boys* are only doing their job. I'll be right back. It's only going to be a brief interrogation."

One of the soldiers decided to place his rifle on the floor, but the butt landed within an inch of Danuta's foot.

"How dare you, you scum," she shouted. "Did you want to hurt me too? Are you going to hit defenseless women now?" Then she turned to the leader and unleashed a tirade of insults he was not prepared for. This pert and normally calm woman had become more than they had expected.

Lech's quick action prevented further difficulties from developing. He quickly put on his hat and coat and embraced his wife in an attempt to calm her. "Honey, please," he pleaded, "I'll be back shortly. Take care of the children and keep supper on the stove for me."

In an instant they were gone. Danuta rushed to the window and continued her vocal attack on the militia from the window. "You vermin, how could you take a father away from his children? You took a man away from me who's been home barely three weeks. How much blood do you want? You are sons of the devil. Your mothers would be ashamed of what you have done here today."

A woman passerby in the street looked up at Danuta and at what was taking place. She became a participant, willing or not, because Danuta began to repeat to her everything she had said before. I'm sure everyone else in the neighborhood could hear also. The car with Lech and four militiamen, and another car with others, quickly disappeared around the corner.

With Lech gone, Danuta turned her fury on Dziadek. "Some bodyguard! You stood there, doing nothing. Why didn't you put up a fight? Why didn't you show them your strength?" Stanley Walesa, sitting in the corner with Hank, got the next tirade.

"And you, dear brother. All talk and no action. Why didn't you come to your brother's defense? How could you sit there and not say something?"

Zbygniew was next.

"What kind of respect did you give your leader today? You had your chance to show your allegiance today. Why didn't you rise to the occasion?

"Do you men want women to do men's work?"

"My God, what's happening? My poor dear Lech. My poor Lech, poor Lech." Emotions gave way to tears and there was silence except for Danuta's sobbing. For a minute it seemed that we were all useless human beings. Then her composure returning, Danuta went back into the kitchen to heat up water for tea. We were all told to sit down, have some tea and contemplate the day's events. We sat there, obedient, helpless and frustrated. Hank disappeared into the bedroom, upset, as we all were. It was ten thirty a.m.

I returned to the study where the scene had taken place and relived those moments. My eye caught the camera on the windowsill and I cursed myself for not snapping a picture of that scene. Damn it, the world would liked to have seen that picture. I could have taken it. Coward!

Stanley and Zbygniew came back into the study and continued to look out the window where Lech himself had stood only moments before.

The phone had been disconnected. No one could call in or out. We were isolated from news and out of touch with everyone.

The atmosphere in the Walesa home became tense. We could only speculate on what was happening. Stanley Walesa was the first to speak, "Well, I'm still going ahead with my plans to be at the monument." Zbygniew added, "You can count on me to go also."

I turned to the same window where Lech had stood and I pondered the events of the day. In my reflections, Danuta's behavior was the most vivid to me. She had attacked the intruders with some of the most abusive language I had ever heard. I remembered words like "snake," "dog," "rat," "shameful behavior," "traitors to your country," "cowards," and "like frightened rabbits." I recalled the fear I'd felt. Although the weapons were not drawn, their appearance inside this home had put a cowardly distance between me and Lech. I felt embarrassed by my behavior. Should I have chanced taking a picture at that moment? Should I have said something? Would there ever be accord between the government and the workers? Could the Russians ever provide a way out for the Poles?

I looked out the window. It was a gusty day. The wind whistled in from the Baltic. I began to wonder what kind of day it was back in the United States. Was this same wind ultimately beating against its shores? Now and then there was a

Lech, Danuta, a friend, and four of the children take a walk in the woods.

Danuta and Lech share a private moment. Danuta was expecting their seventh child when this picture was taken.

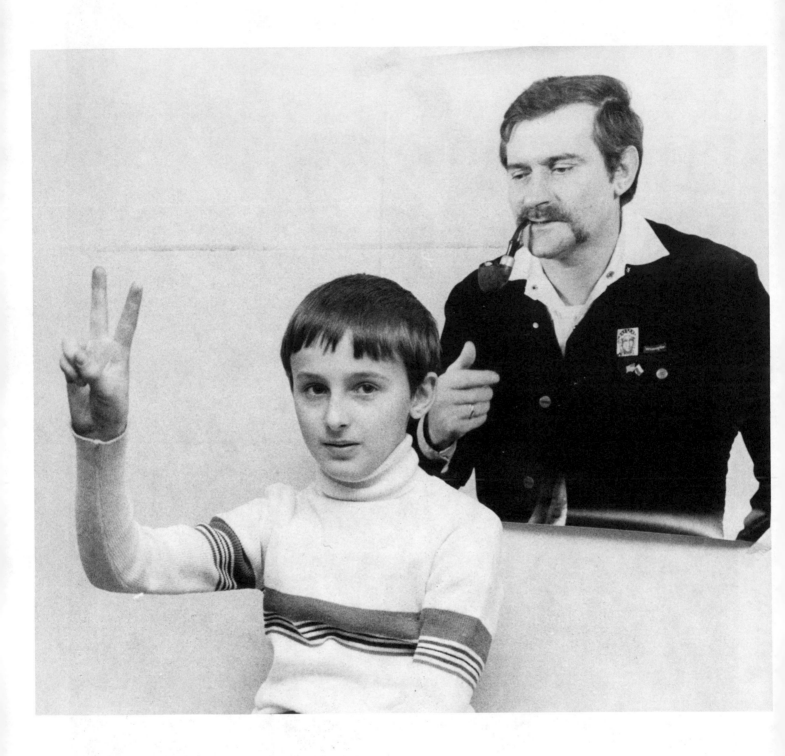

***March 1982. Lech's son Bogdan flashes a
hopeful victory sign before a photo of his
father, who was then in prison.***

***August 7, 1981. Lech shakes hands with
supporters as he leaves a meeting between
Solidarity and government representa-
tives in Warsaw.***

Lech listens to the radio to hear the latest news.

Lech strolls on the beach in the Gdansk neighborhood of Stogi by the Baltic Sea.

snowflake. The day was bright, but overcast. A woman passing by, with a fur collar buttoned tightly around her neck and a fur hat firmly planted on her head, seemed to have difficulty keeping her balance. I caught her eyes looking at Lech's apartment. As she came past the window, she reached for her hat as if to keep it from blowing away. She appeared to be clutching the hat in a strange way, I thought. Then I noticed why—she was displaying the "V" sign with two fingers toward the window. She held that position for about eight or ten paces. No sooner had she passed then a man, in a heavy overcoat and clutching his collar, passed by from the opposite direction. His fingers showed the "V" also. This show of support for Lech was repeated several times by others passing.

I went back to the kitchen to tell Danuta what I had witnessed. She was talking out the window to a young man, recounting the morning's events. When I told her what I had seen, she told me to look out these windows. About two or three minutes later, first two and then three young men passed by, and when they were opposite the apartment they boldly raised their arms to show the "V" sign. "The people know, they have not forgotten, God bless them," she said. "They're all good and brave, but what can they do? We're still under the military, no matter what Jaruzelski said on Monday." (On December 13th, General Jaruzelski had appeared on public television and announced he was lifting 80 percent of the military control in Poland.)

I saw two more men passing by, waving and smiling at the windows. Danuta noticed too, and waved back. She continued to stare out the window now, while peeling carrots and washing potatoes. She recognized a man outside lingering and quickly opened the window to recount the whole story of Lech's visitors. Her emotions were reaching another high as she began to say things like, "He was kidnapped," "He's a prisoner again," "One of them almost hit my foot with the rifle butt," "They were all armed against one defenseless man." I felt myself squirming, wondering if there was any danger in this public exchange. Her voice was rising from excitement.

Dziadek walked into the room and begged her to come away from the window. "You're going to catch cold, dear one. Come away from there. You've had your say, now come away. Besides, that man should not stay there any longer. They might pick him up for questioning too. Dear one, I beg you."

I returned to the study where Stanley and Zbygniew were discussing plans about going to the monument. They asked if I were going to join them. I went to consult Hank about the trip and had forgotten he had gone to our bedroom. I found him asleep, but my stirring in the room awakened him. He made it clear that he would not go to the monument and suggested I should not go either. I had an urge to see this "crisis location." Although I did not plan a confrontation with anyone, I was curious and would have liked to have seen some history in the making.

I looked out the window, it was still windy and raining lightly. Without Lech, some of the motivation to stand out in the cold was gone. I sensed that Hank was nervous about my going when he said, "What am I going to tell Mom if you get detained or arrested?" I went back to the study and told Stanley and Zbygniew we would not attend. They understood, and in five minutes they left for their long walk to the city center.

I got fidgety and a little angry with myself for not thinking of a way to be there and see the activity. I began to examine Lech's library. One shelf contained books on the history of Europe, Poland, and the church. There were at least three books on parliamentary procedures and rules for conducting meetings for large groups. One book had a paper marker sticking out the top. The title of the book was *The Unification of the Catholic Church in Central Europe*. My fingers quickly went to the marker. It was on pages 152 and 153. I began to read eagerly, looking for the reason. There it was next to the last paragraph on page 153, a sentence that mentioned during Medieval times a leader named Caesar Walesa gave an edict to various officials for the purpose of promoting religious unification. It was another strange coincidence, the kind, that often lead to legend and inevitable exaggerations.

Lech had mentioned that strange stories were building up around him already. Someone had told him that in the basement of one church a certain "Lord Walesa" was buried in a vault. In the treasure room at Our Lady of Czestochowa I had seen myself the portrait of a "typical" Polish worker painted before he was known. I had seen this resemblence myself. It was uncanny.

He had made reference to these legends the week before in a toast at the kitchen table: "To the next legend, Polish or Russian." We laughed then, and now I understood better the humor of that remark, I was glad for the diversion of my thoughts. This day had gloom enough.

My attention turned to the beautiful sculptures on the shelves below and above. Here were a standing Madonna carved from a solid piece of coal, a superbly crafted dish made from coal with many religious symbols, a Madonna in wood from France, a St. Jude (I think) from Italy, and a wood carving from Japan. On the top shelf were busts of a famous Polish general and another of

**All goods are in short supply in Poland;
here Lech waits in line to buy cigarettes.**

Lech carved in coal. Unbelievable. Another general and Polish leader, Joseph Pilsudski, had a special corner to himself. I could feel the emotion and the symbolic value of these mementos and books, the value they would now always have for thousands of people. I suddenly felt hesitant about touching them and wondered if it would have Lech's approval. As if she had received a telepathic message from me, Danuta walked into the room to ask if I would come into the kitchen for lunch. She sensed my interest in the books and quickly said, "Did you know he's read every book on those shelves, and some of them more than once. He used to read them on long trips between meetings, before the military intervention. The majority of these books were given to him by teachers, scholars, and lawyers. Now come join us for lunch and return to them later."

Dziadek was already waiting for me to sit down. Ham, liverwurst, pickles, rye bread and tea were served. Crackers with jelly from Germany were our dessert. When I asked if imports were available at the store, Danuta replied, "Don't let anybody tell you that. The shelves are bare and the lines are long. When food comes in, the waiting is agonizing. I'm lucky because Agnes, a family friend, does the shopping for me. God bless her."

"Why is that?" I asked.

"Like Lech, I feel like a prisoner in my own house. You see, if we were to go out in public, we would encounter friends, acquaintances and other interested parties who would want to know about events, the union, the government, Lech's opinions, and what out plans are for the future. As soon as a group of five or more gather, the police come and ask quistions and want your papers. Innocent bystanders become involved. Therefore we must avoid public encounters. An exciting world we have here, don't you think, my cousin?"

The doorbell rang. It was Danuta's doctor coming to see if Danuta was distressed over Lech's absence. "I heard about them coming for Lech and became alarmed about you if he were interned again," she said. She was a staff physician from the area general hospital. She immediately went into a private conference with Danuta in another room just as Danuta's Aunt Helena came to visit. She, too, was concerned about Danuta and the children's welfare.

As we chatted with Dziadek it began to rain more steadily. I wondered where Lech was and how Stanley and Zbygniew were making out at the monument.

Fifteen minutes later, Danuta returned with the doctor and introduced us formally. The doctor was able to speak to us in English and we exchanged stories and discussed some places she had visited in New York, Pennsylvania, and Illinois. Then everybody was tested for their blood pressure. Mine was still normal. I was amazed. The doctor had mentioned that a staff member, on the way to the hospital, had seen Lech in a Mercedes with uniformed men inside. The entire hospital soon became a rumor house of speculation on Lech's situation. It was to have been an important day for Lech and the public. Lech had made it known that he would make his position known to the world on this day.

It was five o'clock. The doctor left when she was satisfied that Danuta's spirits were holding up. Everyone in the room was confident that Lech would return the same day, that it would be a very temporary detainment, timed to tarnish Lech's image and sabotage his attempt to resume his public position.

Danuta became talkative. She asked what type of food we normally ate at home. It seemed clear that she was a little nervous and that just chatting would help pass the time. Stanley Walesa came back alone from his day at the monument. It was 6:45. He joined us at the table and told us of his day's activity. There were militia and ZOMO everywhere. The crowd dropped to several hundred people, but even they were dispersed by the police. Whenever more demonstrators came, they were turned back two blocks before the monument. Stanley and Zbygniew stood or walked around for three hours, always coming back to the monument location to see if they could join anyone or anything at the monument site. Zbygniew finally decided he would return home. Drenched and tired, he bid Stanley farewell and repeated his support for Lech, if ever he should need him.

Stanley told us how he had wandered through the Gdansk streets and how he had met many small groups in doorways and parks. They were waiting for someone to signal or recall them. Anticipating a gathering on this day at the monument, they were reluctant to break up. Stanley repeated to everyone he met the events of the morning and Lech's departure.

Stanley conjectured that Lech would not return until the six-thirty novena service was over at St. Brigida's, the church of Father Jankowski, former Solidarity Union chaplin.

At exactly seven-thirty the doorbell rang and Lech entered. He was moaning from exhaustion. He went directly to his wife, kissing and embracing her, then asked, "Is there any food left?"

"Why should I have something waiting? After all these hours?" A pause. "Sit. Just sit, you fool," she joked.

"Please, honey, don't kid with me. I'm starved. I haven't eaten since I left you," Lech pleaded.

"Just sit down and be still. It's right here," she said. "It's been ready since two o'clock, and it would have been waiting all night even if . . .". She trailed off.

Lech sat, but immediately gave a yell, "Ouch", I can't sit down, I can't. The idiots forced me to ride in their Mercedes sedan for at least five and a half hours. We rode all over Gdansk, from one end to the other. There were two in the front and two in the back. With me in the middle sitting over the hump. Every dip in the road was torture. I tell you, a little longer and I would have agreed to anything." He stood as he began to eat.

"But why didn't you exchange seats with one of them?" Danuta demanded.

"Fat chance. They were afraid I might jump from the car. Honey, I saw every part of Gdansk at least three times, and some streets for the first time."

The food was on the kitchen counter and Lech was devouring everything in reach.

"Take your time, Lech," Danuta added sympathetically. "There's more where that came from. Have some honey with your tea."

Then Lech came around the counter and kissed Danuta, saying, "You're always ready and waiting, aren't you? As usual, anything you touch has that special flavor and pleasure. Thank you, dearest."

Danuta admonished him once again, "Try to sit, Lech. I don't like you to eat standing up." She placed a pillow on the bench, but his discomfort still apparent from the moan he let out. Hank retrieved a foam pad from the study and placed it over the pillow. Lech was still not comfortable, but he was able to tolerate this special assist. "Thank you, Hank," he said as he continued to enjoy his food, which was moved to the table.

As we watched the scene I felt like an intruder, but I wanted to know everything that had happened. This was part of history. I snapped a few pictures. The conversation continued.

"You know, when you get close to them they are not the bad boys you think."

"What do you mean?" I asked. "Aren't they tough and unreasonable?"

"It's a matter of business and survival, as long as you're being watched. But you can't force anyone to do something against his will, to do something that goes against the grain. We drove around for five and a half hours. I never thought a Mercedes could be so tight. After the initial 'sightseeing' I turned to

December 16, 1982. Lech reflects on the hours ahead when he will make a speech at the workers' monument in Gdansk. Just a few minutes after this picture was taken, he was abducted by the police, who took him on a nine hour ride that prevented him from making that speech.

Lech and Danuta relaxing at home.

more personal conversation, about families, education, and the future. You see, they have aspirations too. They long for the same things everyone else wants—time for sports, movies, a place in the country, a vacation abroad, and a good salary to secure comfort in old age.

"As relaxed as we became, whenever something in the distance appeared to hint at a possible crisis they quickly reminded me of their responsibilities and diligence on their job.

"Someday they will all be working for the people and they know it." He smiled at his little joke.

It was eight thirty. The phone was still out of order. Lech was exhausted, but he shifted his attention to some packages and mail that were unopened. "Let's take a look at what we have today," he said suddenly. "Look, here are some letters from America. Tell me, Walt, what do they say?"

"How many letters or packages do you get in a week?" I asked.

Stanley Walesa interrupted, "Ask him how many he gets in a day."

"I get fifty to seventy five pieces of mail daily and two or three packages a day. They come from all over the world. There are many generous people out there. Many thoughtful and compassionate people. People send food, clothing, books, appliances, and even toys for the children. It's been this way since August 1980.

"Before the crackdown we had one hundred times that much each day. Everything had always been distributed by a union committee which saw to it that those in greatest need were served first. Today I share these gifts with friends, co-workers and family. There are so many good people out there whom I wish I could thank personally.

"We've received letters with prayers, greetings for birthdays and Christmas, and hope from many well-wishers. I tell you, brother, I have had my hopes and spirit continuously sustained by these letters. I have faith in the renewal in our government because good people, unafraid and courageous, will make it happen."

"What is the most unusual package you ever received?" I asked

"It came the week before I was released—two cans of Polish ham from France. You must realize that our production of ham is limited in this country."

"What is the most appreciated?"

"I guess, because my wife and children were never able to do normal shopping, especially when the shortages demand good timing at the stores, the variety of clothes my wife and children have received. Whatever does not fit or is something we already have we give away to needy friends and relations. I think it's immoral to hoard.

"Do you get much from the United States?" I asked.

"Do I ever! Let me tell you this, my brother. If I had to thank each sender from the States, I would have to spend a year just shaking hands with those beautiful people. I beg you, please, when you have the opportunity, please thank everyone in America for all their generosity."

"Do you think you'll ever get the chance to visit us in America?" I asked.

"I have high hopes for this summer," he said.

I left Stanley and Lech to their "surprise" packages, bidding everyone good night. It was ten o'clock. As I dug under the covers I heard Danuta's voice demanding an end to this full day. The nine-hour detention was over and Lech was back, feeling none the worse for wear. I heard Stanley saying, "God bless this house and all in it, Lech. Good night."

Lech's response was, "Quiet or you'll wake the whole house. No snoring either, or you'll wake my American brothers."

The translation of the inscription is:
"To my brother Brolewicz"
Ink sketch by Cecilia Cieckiewicz

CHAPTER 6
MY SECOND VISIT TO POLAND

I returned to Poland alone on March 6, 1983. The weather was perfect. It was chilly and sunny. The temperature was a comfortable 36 degrees.

In sharp contrast to my first visit three months before, I presented my five pieces of luggage at customs and was told that I could pass through without inspection. I made a declaration of all items valued at twenty five dollars or more, and a courteous, attractive customs lady smiled and bid me a sincere welcome.

I passed through the gate and was surprised to find myself greeted by six Walesas—Edward, Stanley, Izabela, Thadeusz, Zygmunt and Wojciek. Iza, who had met me alone three months earlier, apologized, needlessly, that Lech was not there to greet me as well. There were the traditional flowers and kisses. I was hugged, patted and squeezed in what became a circle of family warmth and greetings. I could not hold back my tears. We stood there for at least ten minutes, sharing and reuniting family ties.

We then went directly to Iza's home, where she had, of course, prepared a large dinner. Marek and Marzena, her son and daughter, were putting finishing touches on the food when we arrived. The house was filled with laughter and cheers. There were many toasts and many questions.

On this second journey to Poland, I had brought with me the remainder of their parents' belongings. This seemed a perfect time to distribute the numerous personal effects and religious articles and make the small cash distribution that was to go to each. By previous arrangement, at Lech's request, his share was donated to the church.

I showed them photographs I had taken on my previous visit. I also distributed a collection of jeans, shoes, shirts, and sweatshirts from my daughter's college, ladies dresses, underwear, hats, gloves, coffee, chocolates, shaving kits, balloons for the children, silk stockings, baseball caps, and pocket calculators for each family.

The next morning, March 7, I arranged for a taxi to take me to Lech's apartment in Gdansk. It was my third trip to his home.

We arrived at Lech's home about four o'clock. Waiting at the door was Dziadek and Lech. And behind them were Danuta, Mietek, and three of the children—Magda, Anna, and Wiktoria. They made me feel at home and I knew Mom would have been happy about my warm welcome in Poland.

After supper we relaxed in the study and talked. It was as though nothing had changed. The phone kept ringing and the doorbell rang about once every hour, followed by Lech's typical response: *"Mama mia,* I wonder who that is."

Lech was still a heavy cigarette smoker. His hair had been neatly trimmed this time, and he looked well groomed. When I commented on his grooming he replied, "This time I made sure you would not upstage me."

"When do you think the martial law restrictions will be relaxed?" I asked.

"Probably sometime after the Pope's visit in June," Lech replied.

"And you can bet not before then," chimed in Mietek. "You see, they hold this papal visit over our heads. If we make a move of any sort, they might threaten to cancel the visit."

Lech nodded. "You must see our hands are tied, we want to make a move to restore our rights, release all union prisoners and give us back our voice in the government, but they hold this visit like a sword at my throat. Nobody wants to play 'underground,' but we are forced into a clandestine game."

Mietek said, "Did you know that the underground Solidarity has been around so long that they have an underground anthem? To the same tune as 'Jeszcze Polska Nie Zginela' (Poland's national anthem) they sing this verse:

"Poland has not perished
As long as we are holding out here,

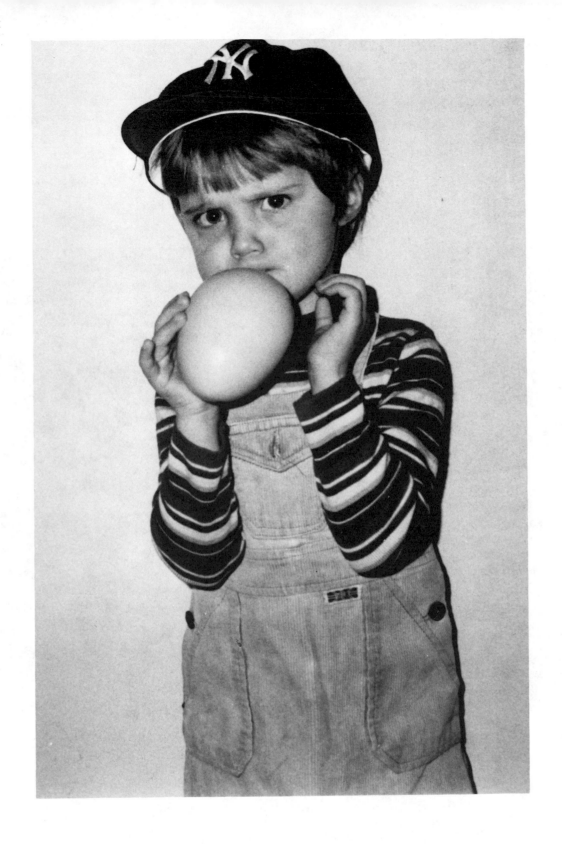

*Magda wears one of the Yankee baseball
hats sent to the Walesas by the publishers.*

Lech in consultation with Father Jankowski.

We shall fight our way to freedom
With the cross and the strikes;
Lead us, Walesa
From the seacoast to Silesia
Polish Solidarity will go on
and win victory."

"We can't go on like this. A whole new culture is developing. Our children are affected by all this. A generation is growing up with a culture of suspicion, distrust and even revolution. Did you know the kids play 'Solidarity versus Police' games, they draw Solidarity symbols on blackboards, papers, and under the chairs of teachers and school officials. The children see their parents in distress and they take to the streets and play games about it. One day I came upon a group of seven or eight children who were being dispersed and chided by a mother. She told me the kids were playing 'waiting in line', pretending they had to line up for shoes and candy, like big people do.

"Father Jankowski told me," Lech said, "that mothers are alarmed over their children's behavior. Five and six-year-olds are using strong language in public places about ZOMO, Jaruzelski and the government. I heard a story recently about a group of kids who stripped a younger boy of his clothes down to his underwear. They were playing customs agents confiscating illegal documents. God help us when these kids grow up. There will be more dissidents than we have now."

So it was true. Earlier this year I had read just such an account in the *Wall Street Journal* about the strain of the Polish ordeal on Poland's children.

I turned to Lech and asked: "So all right, but tell me what can you do about this, my brother?"

"My goal is for Poland to be Poland," he said. "I have been asked by vote to lead this movement and I intend to keep the movement together, legally or not. I know we've quarreled and fought each other, but I intend to make us stand together. It will be my job to keep the movement tight and strong. I will lean on people who are wise and expert in all matters. I will choose the best ideas after discussing them in a democratic manner. Specific problems will be solved by specialists in that field.

"Look, let me put it another way. If I lost today it's only because I lost physically as a man. But the idea, whatever happens later, may prove to be a greater victory."

Lech and fellow Solidarity leader Ardzey Gwiazda talking to workers at the Lenin shipyard in Gdansk.

Lech is jubilant after the departure of Deputy Premier Jaglieski. This was the first victory for the striking workers at the Lenin shipyards.

"Lech," I asked, "don't you think the union also tried to do battle in voices that were too militant?"

"Yes, of course. We were at the brink of revolution, which was brought on in part by the almost hopeless state of the economy. After thirty years of unfulfilled promises by the Communist Politburo, the workers had had enough. Their incentive to work had dried up. They had nothing to show for their efforts. I can still remember during the first Solidarity congress that there were so many strong anti-Soviet statements it nearly caused military intervention by the Soviet Union."

Mietek added, "Also, our economic problems were acute in 1980, and the moderate voices, as well as Lech's own, were weakening within Solidarity. The militant majority were provoking a hard line on the part of the Polish Government and the Soviet Union. Both sides' positions became so hardened that a way out of the crisis seemed impossible."

"And then our members voted for worker support in 1981 in other Soviet bloc countries. This must have been very irritating to the Soviets and our own Politburo," Lech said.

Mietek added, "We just simply took a line from their own book, which urges proletarians everywhere to unite."

I then asked, "If either of you could say, in a single word, what destroyed the union, what would that be?"

"Democracy," Lech shot back.

"Ahh, yes, you hit it right on the head Lech," Mietek said.

"Democracy?" I asked, somewhat surprised.

"Yes, brother, democracy. If this union were going to function fairly and survive, it would have to be through the democratic process. So the majority rule, the right of each voice to be heard and the wish for truth to be heard, no matter how painful, became our downfall."

"That, Walter, was the voice of Solidarity," Mietek closed.

March 8, 1983. I rose, dressed and went to the kitchen. Przemek and Bogdan were just finishing breakfast. They excused themselves and thanked their mother very sweetly and with more courtesy, I thought, than usual.

Lech walked in just as they were hugging Danuta and looked on approvingly. Then it was his turn and Danuta got three extra kisses with a "God love you, dearest." We all sat at the table. Turning to me he asked, "Do you celebrate a day for the ladies in America, Walter?"

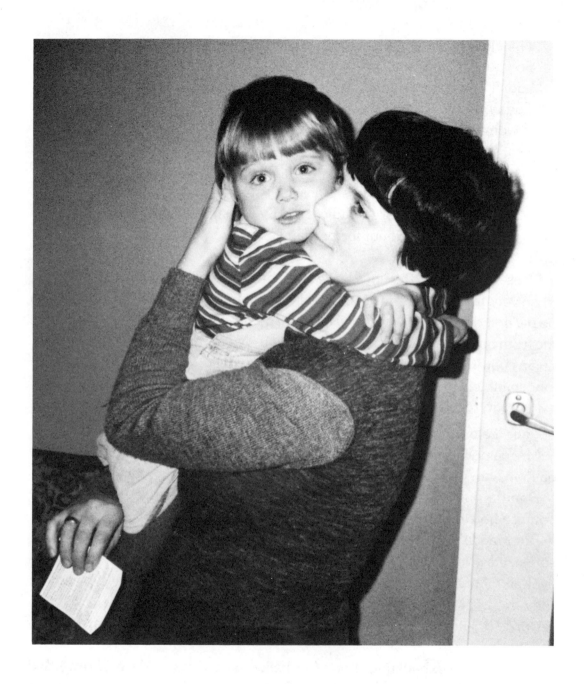

Magda gets a hug from Danuta.

"The closest we get to it is Mother's Day."

"So you don't respect ordinary women?"

"I don't understand."

"Today, my brother, is Ladies' Day in Poland. Today everyone in Poland gives woman her due."

"Yes, but it only happens once every year," Danuta clarified. "All ladies are usually given a holiday from work after lunch, and all day long there are symbols and offerings—flowers, signs in the shops, special attention at public events, and dedications on radio and TV. Just wait and you will feel its presence as we go to Sopot for our family holiday."

"Sopot?"

"Yes, today, after the boys leave for school, we will all go to the market for fresh vegetables and then go for a walk on the boardwalk at Sopot. It will also be my first day of leisure with my family in public. I have asked my aides to free me from business matters today. I invite you, Walter, to join us for this holiday. I want you to go back and tell my aunt, so that she won't think I have been inhospitable."

"I'm flattered, Lech. I only hope I have not already interfered with too much of your life during my stay."

Magda now broke into our conversation, demanding, "Uncle, please fix my balloon, can you fix my balloon?"

Danuta quickly admonished her. "You're a troublemaker, Magda. Can't you see how discourteous you are?"

But Magda's charm completely disarmed me as she took one of my hands, squeezed it and then hugged my leg. "Please, uncle, please, the others are broken." Anna rushed in also and climbed onto my lap. "Yes, please, please . . . they cried." Now they were both in my lap and my arms. "Only if I get a kiss as a reward," I said, "after I inflate each one. Promise?" Each youngster was a delight.

After several exhausting efforts (six balloons) and many kisses, I rewarded each one with a Yankee baseball cap. These caps had been given to me by a friend in the United States.

The kitchen became too close, so I took my "toys" to the study with the children. Many minutes and a dozen balloons later, we joined in a balloon bouncing game. Pretty soon we were all on the floor sitting in a large circle passing the balloons around. We did this for about a half hour, with Lech himself finally joining in with one-year-old Wiktoria in his lap. The excitement

Magda and Anna give me some big smiles.

Because it is the only one of its kind in Poland, Lech's Volkswagen van is easily recognized; people often decorate it with symbols of Solidarity.

Lech, Danuta, two friends, and some of the children take a relaxing walk on the beach just two days after Lech was abducted and prevented from speaking at the workers' monument by police.

with these newfound toys grew to a noisy pitch. Danuta broke us all up, reminding Lech it was now time to go.

We dressed and headed for the car, a Volkswagen van purchased before the military intervention. There were Lech, Danuta, Dziadek, Magda, Anna and myself. Wiktoria was left with a babysitter, Danuta's sister, who came by to help.

Once inside the van, Lech immediately turned on the police band wavelength, searching for a signal. He was rewarded by a voice through the radio transmitter: "There are four big ones and two little ones coming your way. The fox is with them."

"Did you hear, my brother?" Lech said. "You could never be safer, because our 'CIA' is looking after us."

As we took off on the main street I looked back and identified three men in another car following us. It was a strange feeling, but I must admit exciting.

Lech took us for a tour through other parts of Gdansk. A section devoted to townhouses. Not very modern but well kept and maintained. Each street seemed neat and tidy. Now and then Lech would acknowledge a person waving to him. His van, the only one of its kind in Poland, was instantly recognized. More and more people stared, and I could feel their spirit reaching Lech.

Always about 50 to 100 feet behind, our ever-present companions shadowed us cautiously. Their voices, monitored in our van, relayed information to others in the area about our position.

"Walter", Lech asked, "what do you know about our Polish king Walter Sobieski?"

"Let me see," I began, searching my memory, "my Polish history lessons at St. Anthony's School taught me that he was once the hero of all Europe. He saved the entire European continent from the Turkish invasion."

Danuta applauded. "So he is not forgotten in America either," she said.

"Well, then," Lech continued, "did Maciej show you his statue at the entrance to Old Town?"

"Yes," he did, "but it was too dark to see it clearly."

"Well, we are approaching the statue now," he said. The van slowed in the plaza circle so that I could appreciate it better. I insisted that he stop so I could take a picture. "Get out of the car and get up close for a better shot," Lech insisted.

The Walesas on holiday in the seaside town of Sopot.

**Shortages result in the empty stores that
line the busy walks in Sopot.**

It was an impressive monument. I took several pictures. We left before Lech's van became conspicuous. People were beginning to stop and notice who was in the van. As we left the circle, many people waved the "V" sign. Lech smiled and nodded.

We drove for about two miles and entered Sopot, a seashore resort on the Baltic Sea. The houses were small and the streets quaint. The van was parked on a side street and we walked to an esplanade section. It was a beautiful setting for a summer day, even though this was March. Oversized hedges almost twelve feet tall formed the outer ring of a circular walk. The inner circle was ringed with twelve-foot-high pines. There was a beautiful two-story building which, Danuta claimed, was built for a nobleman as a resort home and now served as a tourist information center. There were park benches everywhere.

The boardwalk itself was approximately two blocks long and well maintained. In the water were geese, ducks, swans and seagulls, about one hundred of them in this one section. As we strolled, I couldn't help notice how people acknowledged Lech's presence. There were words of encouragement such as "Keep the spirit," "Hang on Lech," "God bless you," "Don't forget us," "You're not forgotten, Lech." Sometimes there was a discreet "V" sign, and other times just a tip of the hat. No one stopped him to make social conversation. A few words might be exchanged while strolling, without missing a step.

A woman came up to Lech, with apologies to Danuta, and presented him with three roses, saying, "On Ladies' Day, dear Lech, from all women to you."

"I'm happy for you and your objective, Lech," I said. "But isn't it dangerous for people to openly court your leadership role again?"

"Walter," he replied, "what you are witnessing is the true revolution of the masses of my generation. Everyone wants a voice in human freedom. There's a fire burning inside of us. These flowers are the arms of our revolution. We only . . ."

"Lech, please, not now," Danuta pleaded, "this is a holiday for me and your cousin."

"You're right, dear, and I apologize to both of you." Then, turning to me, he said, "Look at this beautiful sandy beach. You should be here in the summer."

I began to notice that most women were wearing or carrying flowers. Ladies' Day was a beautiful gesture by a country that loves anniversaries and holidays. I found myself getting caught up in this holiday, and wished Danuta a happy

Ladies' Day with a bouquet of roses.

We returned to the van and headed back to Gdansk, making one more tourist stop at the Oliwa Cathedral, which is in Adam Mickiewicz Park (honoring the great Polish poet) in Gdansk.

The park was very well planned, with many paths, tree-lined and shrubbed, a duck pond, a botanical garden, an outdoor theater for summer concerts and plays, and the cathedral of Oliwa. The cathedral dates from the twelfth century and is filled with many historical treasures.

The Oliwa cathedral boasts one of the largest pipe organs in Poland. Public demonstrations of the organ's tone and range are offered each day from 10 a.m. to 3 p.m. We arrived at the cathedral about 3:30 p.m., but when the Monsignor, Father Mieczyslaw Gozdziewski, met us walking onto the grounds he arranged for a special demonstration on behalf of Lech and myself.

Pieces by Handel, Bach, Chopin and Szymanowski were played. The most eye catching selection came at the end, when a medley of folk songs were played and Lech reminded me to "Watch the twelve angels, keep watching them, please."

The organ was framed with so many ornate designs it was difficult to pick out the angels, but they were the figures holding trumpets.

In the final folk song, the background lighting became brighter, the arms and bodies of the angels began to move, and the music became louder and more intense. The angels were trumpeting. It was a beautiful and very impressive spectacle.

At the conclusion, someone came to our pew and asked if Lech would agree to be introduced to a visitor from England who had spotted Lech in the church. Lech agreed, but only after he had taken me on a tour of the cathedral. He said it was important to tour the rest of the church while the mood of the organ recital was still with us.

He was right. Behind the altar were many religious treasures: fine works of art sculptured from wood and marble, a vault crypt where famous members of the church were buried, and delicately wrought stations of the cross. Throughout the church much reconstruction was being delayed awaiting renewal funds.

As we completed our tour and returned to the front of the church, there was a group of five or six people waiting there patiently. Their tour guide came over to us and asked if Lech would greet his anxious English tourist. The tourist turned out to be a cousin of the queen of England, accompanied by her niece

Father Gozdziewski, Lech and myself at the entrance to the Oliwa Cathedral in Gdansk. The cathedral suffered damage during WW II, as can be seen from the crumbling bricks.

A Christmas celebration at the Walesa's.

Lech exchanges views with a friend, Mietek, and Father Jankowki. The flowers are a Ladies Day present to Danuta.

and husband. She was most interested in what Lech and the Solidarity spirit had done in Poland. Everyone was most friendly and cordial. The Queen's cousin expressed her private feelings about Lech's role in the future, hoped he would stand firm and continue to act as the peoples' voice. We returned home shortly afterward and found Mietek waiting. The holiday was over.

No sooner had we finished our supper than the doorbell signaled more guests. Three friends had come by to draw up plans for an upcoming event. Five minutes later and Father Jankowski and an aide joined the growing group in the study. The room became filled with much chatter about the event. I was amazed to hear Lech holding three separate conversations. His staccato sentences drew reactions from the others that seemed to signify their satisfaction. They were standing or sitting around him, or frowning down at him, discussing problems.

I was struck with how there did seem to be a fox like quality to his appearance. He communicated with a sense of quickness, manipulating the conversation until extreme positions were reduced to a compromise. He seemed to adore the business of negotiating issues. People used him to bounce off ideas on critical issues and always came away with some sense of relief. Lech was in his element. No one in the room could match his electricity. I could feel him sending currents between himself and his audience, as he had so often done with me. Lech once told me, "I'm more at home with trouble than with peace. I am a troublemaker in search of compromise. The door must always be slightly ajar for negotiation. Poles must talk things out with Poles."

The conference covered all kinds of confidential matters. As interested as I was in the exchanges, I was content to just look at their attempts to conduct the talks on the level of a whisper. I had been told that Lech's apartment and phone were monitored.

Throughout the discussions the phone continued to ring, tea and cookies and chocolates were served, and ashtrays were emptied. Added to this confusion were radio broadcasts from America and London (just in case there was some critical news). Before and after the news, Lech played my classical and popular tapes from America.

After the company had left, Lech and Mietek invited me to join them on a trip to Grudziadz the next day to attend the trial of Anna Walentynowicz, who was being tried for a violation of martial law. I said that I would like very much to join them.

For the final hour before 11 p.m., the day's mail was examined. I was drafted to help translate the English language correspondence. There was a good deal of it—Easter cards and well-wishers from Minnesota, Maine, and Ohio, touching and emotional words of comfort and support.

One letter from a Protestant couple in Minnesota suggested that Lech was Poland's new messiah, summoned from obscurity like Joan of Arc. I asked Lech whether he thought of himself as a messianic figure.

"Only God and his Holy Mother would know for sure," he smiled. "I have been at the bottom and will be at the bottom again. If I am to lead the workers in a new voice I shall do it only with God at my side. But even if I achieve this goal, I shall become a nobody again."

CHAPTER 7
THE TRIALS

The next morning after breakfast Mietek arrived and the four of us got into Lech's Polonez, the other of his two cars. Waiting were two police vehicles and two television crews, one from NBC and the other from CBS. There is never any secret about where Lech Walesa is going when he travels, because he makes it clear in his telephone conversations or in conversations in his apartment, usually looking up knowingly at the ceiling. On this day, from their telephone interview the night before, the TV media decided where they wanted to be this morning.

A brief television interview took place outside, next to the car, where Lech again acknowledged he was going to Grudziadz to attend the trial of Anna Walentynowicz as an observer. He wanted to make it clear to Anna that, as a union brother, he supported her activist role. He would be there to reinforce her morale, but in his presence alone.

Once we got out on the highway, one of the police cars took a position ahead of us to "lead" the caravan of five automobiles. The trip took about an hour and a half.

I was excited by all the attention. The strange caravan was of interest to all of us. "But how could the police car take the lead so confidently?" I asked. "How do they know they won't be tricked? What if you stopped all of a sudden at a restaurant? What if ..."

But Lech stopped me. "Listen, my brother, our 'CIA' knows everything. Their vigilance is constant. I only try to make it easier for them."

"What do you mean?" I asked.

"Don't be naive, my brother. My telephone and walls are all ears, so I play the game. Otherwise, the hassling and monitoring would be too frustrating for me. Look, Walter, one of the media crew is waving to us. I think they are taping us. Wave to them."

Sure enough, their camera was pointed at us. Everyone in the car managed some sort of a salutation. Not such a tight control by the military, I thought. Control, to be sure, but less rigid and restrictive than I had assumed.

As the countryside rolled by, I again found broad, beautiful and fertile farmland. What riches, I thought. A land so rich must have a good harvest. Where is all the food? Why all the shortages? What kind of productivity is there? Why isn't agriculture successful here? My curiosity was working again, but I worried that more questions from me might only annoy him.

"Where has all the food gone, Lech?" I asked.

"To the East, for distribution," he replied sarcastically.

"Lech," I started, "would you mind giving me a short history lesson?"

"What do you mean?"

"How did the Solidarity union get started? What were the circumstances that led up to the creation of an independent union?"

"It's a good thing we have a long ride ahead of us and that there is nothing better to do," he said, moaning.

"How did the union organize itself into a single unit. I cannot conceive how all the various sections of the country, spread so far apart and with such diverse interest groups, came to speak with one voice, especially in this political atmosphere."

"I suppose it was on July 1, 1980," he began, "when the government tried again to raise the price of meat—that is what broke the national camel's back. The response was a wave of strikes. For us in Gdansk it was also the firing of Anna Walentynowicz from her crane operator's job. Although the strikes were sporadic at first, they increased in number by early August. It was all unrehearsed. On August 16, 1980, it was a victory for us when we established the first interfactory strike committee. At the time we also represented twenty other striking units as well as the Lenin shipyards.

"There were about eighteen thousand men and women inside the shipyard. The miracle was that it even got started." Lech lit another cigarette and reflected on those moments. "Those workers had decided to strike without any prepared logistics. That morning they brought their lunches from home without realizing how far it might go. The people from the vicinity also went to work. There were no restaurants, no cafeterias or any other food sources inside those gates when they locked themselves in. Our neighbors and people came from the city, baked and cooked and carried food and cigarettes on foot and came on bicycles to us. You see, the buses and street cars were on strike too. As the news spread to other villages, horse carts began to arrive at the docks, loaded with potatoes, cabbage, cheese, and apples. There was even one cart filled with pigs. Although our taxis were not on strike, they pitched in by cruising around the city to provide transportation to anyone bringing food to the strikers. Mingled with the carts were limousines that brought university professors, labor relations experts and advisors who volunteered their knowledge for the welfare of the workers. Our success was achieved by determination and unity of purpose and the realization that we Poles belong together. Where there was fear before to speak out in public, suddenly there was a feeling that we were *all* friends. Everyone felt a new dignity.

But do not misunderstand, these gains were made possible by a series, or rather a unique combination, of the right characteristics, which seeded and gave strength to the free union movement. Our demands reflected longstanding economic grievances and also deep-seated political frustrations of our society as a whole. These frustrations were countrywide. It guaranteed our movement a unity which found its expression in the new union's name: Solidarity. Although I was elected as the new leader, I cannot take credit for the skills of all the other workers' leaders. They displayed exceptional maturity and restraint during those times. Their combined organizational skills prevented violence. Another set of exceptional characteristics was displayed by our receiving the support of the professional intelligentsia (lawyers, doctors, teachers, engineers, for example) and the advisory body of the Committee for the Defense of the Workers (KOR)."

"Would you say that Poland's economic problems were the basis for the unrest?" I interrupted.

"No, no, it's more complex than that. It just can't be summarized that easily. To know the complete answers you must dig deeper to know Poland better. It is true that Poland was, and still is, in an economic crisis and that our demands were economic in nature, but our economic problems were only a symptom and a result of deep-seated political problems."

"Lech," I interrupted again, "are you implying that the Solidarity movement was concerned more with politics than with the usual sort of trade union work?"

"Yes, and it had to be, whether we liked it or not. To get a free and independent trade union we had to deal with the politics of the system. You should also understand that Solidarity represented not only the workers' demands for reforms and new freedoms but also a broad coalition of all social forces and social classes in the country.

Our country's Roman Catholic religion is an integral part of our national identity. It is in conflict with the political system that our government adopted. The postwar settlement of this political system has always been at odds with the majority of the Polish people. Study us more carefully and you will see that the present Polish government is in conflict with our political culture. The system works against our religious identity. No one, so far, has ever succeeded in controlling the independent social force rooted in our church. We have a highly individualistic character; we've always distrusted authority. These characteristics do not fit the socialistic model our government represents. We're not anarchistic. We're willing to give any system a chance."

Our chat was ended because we were now approaching a bridge leading into Grudziadz, and Mietek commented on the presence of more police at the end of the bridge. We had no sooner gotten off the bridge when a police official standing in the roadway motioned us to pull over. Three voices simultaneously muttered, "Damn it." Then Lech added, "They are going to try to delay our arrival at the trial."

We halted and Lech rolled his window down, asking, "What is the trouble here? Aren't we allowed to proceed on this road?"

"Yes," was the response, "but I must first see your papers, please."

"Now, look, please don't bother with that, I'm Lech Walesa and this is my chauffeur, this is my friend, and this is my brother from the United States. We're on our way to watch a trial in this city's courthouse, which will start in about ten minutes."

"I'm sorry, sir, but I must look at your papers," he said.

"This is totally unnecessary. Why don't you look at their papers too?" Lech pointed to the plainclothes policemen in the parked car ahead (the same one from our caravan).

"I don't have to check their papers," the policeman said. "I promise not to be too long. Please let me have your papers," he insisted. So we surrendered our

Lech, Danuta, and two of their children walk to St. Casmir's Church in Gdansk. A crowd of 10,000 people had gathered at St. Brigitte's Church, expecting Lech to attend, but the government warned him against it and he changed his plans.

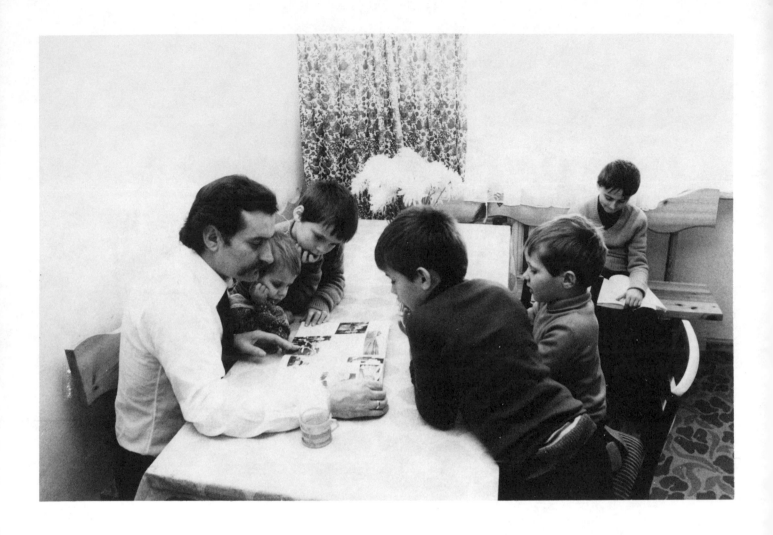

*Lech and some of his children look at a
book written about Solidarity.*

ID papers and wondered how long this detainment would be.

It was only four or five minutes before the policemen returned with our papers and we were allowed to continue. It was a pleasant encounter at that. The policeman's attitude and courtesy were unexpected. We were on our way. At the end of another eight or ten blocks we found the courthouse. Parking was not permitted in front of the building this day, so Mietek dropped us off a few yards from the entrance. We got out of the car to face a small crowd who recognized Lech. Everyone pushed forward to see better. The air was charged with anticipation of a confrontation. We got out of the car with determination and Lech instructed me to stick close to him and move forward. I was about to experience my first encounter with Lech's public.

We took about ten paces toward the building entrance and found ourselves surrounded by about a dozen people. One man came forward, saluted and said, "Success to you, Lech. Keep it up"; and another man, "We are grateful for your coming here"; and another, who made the two-fingered "V" over his heart, just said, "We wait."

There were men with cameras standing across the street snapping our pictures. Lech's elbow nudged mine and he whispered, "CIA". The NBC crew in our caravan began filming us. The crowd pulled in tighter to get close to us, never giving the media a chance for an interview. Lech, on the other hand, kept moving forward. The crowd was giving him just enough room so as not to trip and collide with him. Just then I noticed he was carrying flowers and asked, "Where did they come from?"

"I don't know," he answered.

We got to the door and went up the steps into a crowded hall. Someone pointed to a door where they said Walentynowicz's trial was scheduled. The door was locked, so Lech knocked. A man opened the door and asked for our passes. We were told to go to the director's office for approval.

We turned around and tried to get through a very crowded hallway. There were more flowers; Dziadek was now carrying the surplus from Lech. There were many whispered messages and words of confidence. The "V" sign appeared everywhere. I was beginning to lose my position alongside Lech, when I felt Dziadek's strong hand pull me forward by the arm. At last we came to the director's office and entered his private chambers.

At first the director was agitated, but Lech insisted on our request to get into the courtroom. "Look, I'm here to observe only, and my brother from the United States would like to see our judicial system at work." Lech's charm was like magic in the situation, and we were soon given a signed paper allowing us to enter the courtroom.

The hallway on the way back was now even more jammed. We literally had to push and shove our way through. We got to the courtroom door, knocked, and this time the court attendant allowed us inside. It was a large room with a high dias for three judges, and on the other side a defendant's isolation box with a lawyer's desk in front.

Facing the judges' dias were approximately fifteen rows of benches for spectators. There were about one hundred people already seated. As we approached the spectators' section to find a seat, I was caught off guard when about seventy or eighty of the people stood up halfway and held that position for about three seconds. Everyone was looking at Lech. He waved his arm, as a senior officer might return a salute, and everyone sat down. We headed straight for the last row, where we sat down and waited for the proceedings to begin. I felt proud to be next to Lech and admired how the people exhibited their politics in this quiet way. No hailing, no words, not a sound. This was another example of the unquenchable Polish spirit.

We seated ourselves in the back row and waited for the trial to start. I studied the spectators and caught the eyes and smiles of many who were looking at us too. To the right of the room Lech pointed out to me a few members of the Walentynowicz family. A court administrator announced that the trial was about to begin, and three judges entered and took their places at the dias. The lawyer for the defense stood up and asked the court's permission for some other close members of Anna Walentynowicz's family to attend the trial also. Obtaining permission was difficult because of Anna's special political situation.

Anna Walentynowicz now entered the defense box. There was a flurry of hand waving between Anna and her family when she entered the room and caught sight of them. Anna then scanned the rest of the room, waving now and then to a familiar face. Her face gleamed with excitement at this opportunity to meet the general public again. She had been arrested in November at the Gdansk shipyards for making unlawful speeches about union business, a violation under martial law.

Alone in the box, she looked like a hero from a page in Polish history. Her high cheekbones and square jaw, with its jutting chin, gave her an aggressive appearance. Her turbaned head gave her a military look, but her eyes had a warm and tender depth so characteristic of a woman who had matured through motherhood and hard work.

The judge presented a choice to the defense—whether to begin the trial at once or allow the defense's opening remarks to set the record straight. After a short conference with her attorney, Mrs. Walentynowicz decided to set the record straight.

Mrs. Walentynowicz began a detailed biographical account of her work with the unions, before Solidarity, to justify her congregating with workers and public speechmaking. She pointed out her leadership role and how her fellow workers had come to rely upon her to represent them. Having traveled to Italy, France and Japan, and having been chosen by free elections among her workers, her leadership role was well documented. Thus, by making a public speech in Gdansk she was not creating a disturbance or acting against the government but merely reassuring the workers of her continuing representation during a time of confusion. Her address lasted one and a half hours. A twenty-minute recess was granted before the trial resumed.

We went out into the hall to stretch and have a smoke. The halls were jammed with people. The moment Lech came within sight of the crowd, the crush toward him became uncontrollable. There were autographs, personal messages and questions about Lech's objectives. Reporters from NBC attempted to record an interview, but they were no match for the crowd, which wanted to know more about the union's future and whether Lech would continue his leadership role. Once again I lost my place beside Lech. Dziadek had his hands full to keep Lech from harm and he did that job well, but the pandemonium in the hall was getting worse.

Lech began making his way back to the courtroom just as a bell rang signifying that court would reconvene in two minutes. I was falling further behind and could see Dziadek shoving Lech into the room. Just as I started to think how I might launch an offensive to get through the crowd, Dziadek's large frame loomed in front of me pushing everyone out of the way. He gripped my shoulder and in an instant I joined Lech inside. He was waiting for me at the door.

We resumed our seats and Lech asked, "What did you think of that?" I remarked something about how good it was to have Dziadek around, and Lech added, "Wait till this is finished and we get outside."

"Did you see Mietek?" I asked. "I hope he's not in trouble." But before Lech could answer, the judges returned and the room was hushed.

The superior judge announced that the court was going to study Mrs.

Walentynowicz's address to the court and that time was needed. Therefore, he said, the court would reconvene the last week in March and weigh her emotional and detailed request for a fair ruling.

Lech rushed through the aisle to talk to Anna Walentynowicz before she was taken away, but all he got was a wave from her just as they closed the door. We were not given permission to see her privately. Her family was also denied any private audience. So we turned once again to the exit and the crowd. I heard Lech say once again, before we were swallowed up in the melee, "Stick close to me and don't stop for anybody." I nodded.

The urgent need of the crowd to touch or talk to Lech was without discipline. Dziadek and Mietek were waiting for us in the hall, and they were a welcome sight. We headed for the exit to leave the building, but blocking our path was an NBC television crew. Lech advised me not to stop for an interview but to just keep walking slowly to wherever the car was parked. An American correspondent with the NBC crew caught my ear and asked if I would help them with an interview. Lech's answer to this was, "Only if it is done on the move."

NBC: "What are you doing here?"

Lech: "Attending the trial of Anna Walentynowicz."

NBC: "Are you a witness or a participant in the trial?"

Lech: "I'm simply an observer to give Anna Walentynowicz whatever support she can use."

NBC: "Is it true that Mrs. Walentynowicz was an outlaw in the Solidarity Union?"

Lech: "Mrs. Walentynowicz may have had other objectives for the union than the majority, but she was a loyal supporter nevertheless."

NBC: "Is it true that you and Mrs. Walentynowicz had a falling out, and if so, why are you here now?"

Lech: "We may have had our disagreements, but we were brother members and I'm here to show Mrs. Walentynowicz my moral support, financial support and any other spiritual life I can offer a loyal and faithful union member of so many years."

We were slowing down, so Lech reminded me to keep walking and not to slow down.

NBC: "Do you have anything else you would like to say, Mr. Walesa?"

Lech: "Yes, I would like to say hello to my other brother in New Jersey."

We arrived at the car and the interview was over. We got inside the car just as the crowd surrounded us. Mietek had some fear of moving the car because of the jam. Some people begged Lech to roll down his window. He lowered it about six inches. Cards, flowers and hands came through. Most of them implored him to keep faith and confidence, to keep up his confrontation with the government. One woman pressed her face against the window and asked why he had given up. She began to challenge his faith and asked what the authorities had done to make him lose courage. Before Lech could respond, militia personnel opened a path for our car and we finally got started. We headed for home exhausted and hungry.

CHAPTER 8
GOODBYE TO MY BROTHER

I stayed in bed for about twenty minutes the next morning, thinking about the previous day's events. I recalled the pressure of the crowds around us. The various voices of hope and of criticism. But always the constant attempt by everyone to touch Lech, to be a part of the scene, and finally the courage of their resistance to the authorities and their willingness to violate laws against congregating "unlawfully."

I showered and dressed. In the kitchen Danuta was feeding the children oatmeal. She sat Wiktoria in her lap and spoon fed her. It was a delight to watch her impose discipline over the breakfast table and see the children react. Wiktoria, the youngest, finished breakfast first and Danuta declared her the most cooperative. When Bogdan, aged twelve, was finished he courteously offered to hold the baby while his mother brewed more hot tea.

Lech came in, dressed and shaved. "Well brother, are we ready for another ride?" he asked. "Where to today?" I asked.

"Elblag."

"What's happening there today?" I asked again. "The trial of six young men who were the victims of police brutality."

"What were they charged with?" I asked.

"During martial law, they were caught putting up anti-government posters and distributing literature. While in prison they were beaten and their families filed complaints against the police. Before the trial can proceed their complaints must be answered. I'm only going as an observer to reinforce their families' position. If it pleases you, your company would be welcome."

"Just being with you would make it a privilege to attend!" I answered.

"Done. And now, my dear, have you fed my brother yet? I would not want my aunt to hear of any poor hospitality from your kitchen."

"Sit yourself down, be calm and keep quiet!" Danuta replied.

Mietek came in and joined us. Danuta was kept busy. Mietek remarked how during the heydey of Solidarity the breakfasts on the road were not always so large. Danuta insisted everyone eat as much as they could because it would be a long wait between meals. As we ate, Mietek reminded everyone it would be an hour and a half to Elblag.

We started to Elblag in a mild rain. Outside a CBS TV crew was waiting for us. A brief interview was given and we were off. Once again a caravan of two police cars, TV crew, and our van headed for the open road. As usual, once we were on the highway, one of the police cars assumed a position in front to lead the way. We settled in for the long ride—talking about the United States— traffic in New York,m crime in the big cities, the number of television channels available to watch, the variety of entertainment, and the elections for public office. Mietek was commenting on the strength and weaknesses of our past presidents when Lech interrupted to say how he thought we were fortunate to find a man such as President Ronald Reagan. "Why do you like Reagan?" I asked.

"I've read," he said, "how he is attempting to introduce a program for reducing crime, eliminating cheating in the government and fighting inflation. He comes across having a strong will to win."

Mietek chimed in, "That's our Lech too, a strong will and determination. You've got your Ronald and we have our Lech."

"Listen, Walter", Mietek continued, "there's more to Lech than you know. During that day in August when Solidarity began, Lech's skills of leadership went well beyond the confrontation with management. On the third day of the strike he led the workers of the shipyard away from a quick agreement that would have given the workers generous terms for going back to work and ended the strike there, but left the strikers at other plants without similar terms. Lech insisted everyone continue the strike in solidarity with other workers.

That, Walter, was when the movement for free and independent trade unions got underway."

"In addition," Lech interrupted, "when Solidarity started that August of 1980, we went looking for young leaders spoiling for a fight. We tried to find people who would be reasonable, also, who would be tacticians and strategists and be able to carry on the wider dialogue."

Dziadek added, "Those were tough months on your wife and children, too."

"You're right, dear friend. The Holy Mother has blessed me and especially my Danuta—she has more tolerance and patience than our Madonna," said Lech.

"Excuse me," I asked, "could you describe that moment for me when you 'took over' at the shipyards."

Lech started, "Let's see, that would have been August 14, 1980. When things started to happen at the shipyard, four policemen were posted at my home to watch my every movement the day before. When I heard how things were developing. I slipped away from them and got into the shipyard at a crucial moment. Two thousand workers were having a meeting and the top manager was making promises and asking everyone to leave. Nobody was opposing him and, in fact, most were beginning to leave. This was the moment. My blood was boiling. My emotions were pent-up. I elbowed my way through the crowd and I set myself in front of the manager. I began to shout at him that the workers would not go anywhere if they weren't sure they had obtained what they wanted. Hearing me, the workers began to feel stronger and I became their leader.

"And you still are," Mietek concluded.

"Lech, how else did Solidarity focus on worker benefits? I mean besides the establishment of free and independent trade unions and the right to strike," I asked.

"Well, we demanded freedom of speech, the right to publish the printed word, both of which were always guaranteed by the Polish constitutions, and access to the mass media for persons of all religious pursuasions, which meant we could hear Sunday morning mass over the radio. I think our major point over-all was to focus on human dignity."

"What does that mean?," I interrupted.

"Well a case in point are the Silesian miners. The authorities' approach to those miners was—'Just give them money, and bottles of beer and vodka.'

This approach treated them as though they were sub-human. For example, the miners had a special fund for encouraging miners to work on Saturdays. The miners had to pursuade management to give them less money for overtime. They argued that they were being paid too much to work on weekends. Silesians felt the extra money, four times their normal pay, and special food supplies, somehow dishonored them. They felt the old system of weekend mining was anti-family for Christian men. Reluctantly, management agreed to discontinue this fund."

"You know, Lech," I said, "your stepfather and I know someone in Pennsylvania who works with unions and management in industry, stressing similar ideals and a concept he calls 'value of the person.' He also admires your aims and is anxious to meet you someday."

The city of Elblag came into view and our thoughts turned to the sights of the city. Some of the architecture was uncharacteristic of a Polish city, and for good reason. This used to be a section of Germany, ceded to Poland at the end of the war and formerly known as Elben.

We pulled into a parking place in front of the courthouse building. A big improvement over the restrictions at Grudziadz. About a dozen people milled about the front of the building. It was quiet and peaceful. We got out of the van and stretched.

We entered a hall ornamented with lovely arches made of wood. The marble floor, the fancy handrails made of brass, the bronze art plaques on the walls, and sculptured ceilings all created a classic atmosphere. As we reached the second floor, we saw a hallway crowded with people. Once again we became the center of attention. Lech had Dziadek very close to him. Flowers, words of comfort, and general goodwill greeted Lech everywhere. Mietek quickly found out where approval passes were issued. This time all four of us were authorized to be admitted.

We were about twenty minutes early so we lingered in the hall and enjoyed a smoke, but not without becoming an attraction. A woman came up to Lech for an introduction and a gift of two carnations. A man in his twenties escort an elderly man who had recognized Lech and asked if he could be introduced. His eyes filled with tears while he tried to explain why he could never be active in the Solidarity movement because of his age. In defiance he wore the Solidarity pin (now outlawed) to show his courage. Lech was visibly touched. He kissed the man on his cheek and asked for his prayers to the Madonna to maintain his strength.

A reporter from CBS came over to Lech and began an interview. Always on his guard, Lech was cautious not to be maneuvered into controversial issues. It was a pleasure to watch him spar with reporters. One of the defense lawyers came by and introduced himself. Shaking Lech's hand, he freely admitted his personal allegiance to the Solidarity movement, adding with a smile that his feelings would, of course, be governed by what the state declared to be "legal." A woman carrying a one-year old pushed through and begged Lech to kiss her infant "for luck".

A signal whistle sounded to announce that court was about to convene. We entered the courtroom. Its many windows that let in a lot of light, and the atmosphere seemed open and free. We sat down on the benches and were warned that due to spontaneous applause that had erupted when the defendants entered the courtroom the day before, no outbursts would be tolerated that day.

We sat for about twenty minutes before a court attendant announced that the defendants were about to be brought in. A minute later, the sound of footsteps could be heard and the first defendant entered the prisoners' box. He was wearing a big smile and the others who filed in behind him had similar expressions. Suddenly, their hands shot up in the air with the "V" finger salute. At this moment, Lech himself stood up and facing the defendants made the "V" sign with both his hands raised high in the air. This prompted an immediate reaction from the rest of the audience and there were suddenly about one hundred and fifty people, silent and smiling, standing with their hands raised triumphantly over their heads in symbolic salute to the Solidarity cause. The only sound in the room was a crack from either a loose floorboard or a seat. This silent display lasted only a few seconds. Just as silently and spontaneously everyone sat down again. But the effect on the defendants in the prisoners' box was electric and they were visibly moved and heartened. It was as though an explosion of spirit had engulfed the entire room.

The eight lawyers entered the room and took their places. Three judges followed a few minutes later, and the trial began. Two physicians were presented to give testimony for the government. They placed in evidence medical records they said indicated that three of the defendants had pre-existing injuries and illnesses that could account for the injuries now claimed by them to have arisen from the alleged incidents of police brutality.

The physicians were cross-examined and the defendants then testified as well. After an hour or so the court agreed to hear the closing statements for the defense. The pleas for the defense were lengthy and eloquent. Each defending lawyer presented strong views on the rights of citizens to free speech. The last plea for the defense was presented by the senior lawyer of the group. His speech lasted about an hour and a half. It was an emotional and patriotic delivery filled with references to history, the church, and the sacrifices Poles have always been willing to make. He included stories of other young men who found greatness in the pursuit of principle and the mention of the names of Kosciuszko and Pulaski caught my attention especially, as they are well known to everyone in the United States.

A full five and one half hours after the proceedings began, the judges called for an adjournment to review the evidence and the pleas by the defense. Another date was set to resume the proceedings in about two weeks. The judges left the room. We were, by then, restless, tired, and sore from the hard benches. The long and uninterrupted trial made us hungry and our thoughts turned to where we could find something to eat. Restaurants might be available, but we knew the menus would be limited, at best. Before we could worry much about it, one of the trial lawyers conferred with Lech. It had already been settled. We were all invited, with the attorneys, to have lunch with the pastor of the local church.

We arrived at the rectory in several cars. There were eighteen guests present in all—the lawyers, friend from the trial, and our group. Everyone was exciting that Lech was there. The topics were varied and it seemed that in the hour we spent at the table we somehow touched at least once on every one of the world's problems.

Just as we were finishing our meal, the pastor's mother, who was also the head cook, was introduced to Lech. She carried a flower and a paper bag. The flower, she said, was from her heart, for good health. And the bag was from her kitchen and filled with specially baked babka, for Danuta and Lech's children. We all smiled. Shyly, she asked Lech if she could give him a kiss. Lech, taken himself by the emotion of this moment, responded by embracing her and kissing her cheek to cheek three times. She held his hand and said to him, "Sto lat, Lechu. Jeszcze Polska nie z ginela puki ty z nami." "May you live one hundred years, Lech. Poland is not lost while you are with us." We applauded now, seconding her thoughts with cheering of our own.

We left shortly afterward, with farewells and good luck wishes from everyone. We returned to Gdansk with four additional passengers who had made their way to the trial on their own and needed a ride home.

We got back to Gdansk early that evening. We had been cramped in the van but travel conditions and our weariness did not seem to have an effect on the conversations. With the same curiosity I had about Poland, Lech's passengers asked me questions about the United States: How long do you have to wait for a new car purchase? (In Poland it normally takes years to get delivery.) How high is the unemployment in America? Is it true that Chicago has more Poles than Warsaw? Is there a long wait for apartment housing? (In Poland the wait for housing can also take years.)

I learned that almost every Pole seems to have at least one relative in the United States. The relationship can be either close or distant, but it is enough to make their feeling of closeness to America stronger than I had imagined.

We eventually reached the heart of Gdansk and began to drop off our riders one by one. Just before we were about to cross over the bridge to the Zaspa section where Lech lived, Lech told Maciej to detour slightly and let me have another look at the shipyard monument. Shortly, we were in front of the huge columns that formed the memorial: three slender wooden trunks, 138 feet high, topped by three crosses with an anchor affixed to each. The monument stands just outside of the main gate of the Lenin shipyard.

"This, Walter," said Lech, "was a personal achievement for me. To the memory of so many no longer with us from the 1970 food riots, this monument will stand to remind us of the rights of human beings. For me it embodies the rights of people to their dignity and to justice."

I asked about the anchors at the top of the columns.

"Traditionally, the anchor in Poland is a symbol of hope. I asked that they be put there so that it would symbolize hope which was being crucified," Lech explained.

"Have you seen the sculptured scenes at the bottom, Walter?" Maciej asked.

"No, I was never that close," I responded.

"Well then, let me try to describe it. There were many persons involved in the design, but Lech's influence was the dominant one. At the bottom there are carvings of shipyard scenes, men bolting plates and hammering rivets. Another scene shows women grieving and there is a caption with lines written by Czeslaw Milosz (the winner of the Nobel Prize for literature in 1980.) The line I remember reads, 'You can kill one man but a new one will be born.' "

"And just to be sure, we put a black stone behind the memorial," Lech added, "with the inscription 'They sacrificed their lives so that you can live in dignity.' "

"And below that we have a word from Pope John Paul—'Let your spirit come down and change the face of the earth, this earth,'" Maciej added.

We started up the overhead crossing, driving toward the Zaspa again, as Lech continued. "That was a very happy and emotional moment for me that day. We had all sorts of dignitaries attending. Our president Jablonski, Cardinal Macherski of Krakow, and thousands of people from the party. We observed a minute of silence. Then the city's church bells began to ring and ship sirens wailed from the port. We had the names of those who died in Gdansk and Gdynia in 1970 read aloud at the monument, and after each name the people would shout, 'Yes, he still lives among us.' "

Maciej interrupted. "At the end, Lech lit a memorial flame and offered some words for those in power and those who sacrificed. It touched the hearts of everyone."

"For me the monument stands like a tree with deep roots. Even if it is cut, it will blossom again," Lech concluded.

We were all exhausted by the time we arrived inside the apartment. Lech announced, "I'm home, dear." There was a near avalanche of children rushing to greet him. They swarmed around him, shouting and screaming, "Where were you, Daddy? Where did you go, Daddy? Daddy, did you bring us something?"

To their surprise and mine, he produced lollipops for each. "My little pearls," I heard him say, "were you good children for Mommy? Did you eat what you were supposed to for Mommy?"

With all the noise I could still hear a loud scream from one-year-old Wiktoria, who was having difficulty maneuvering her walker past her brothers and sisters. Lech reached down and picked her up. By that time, Magda and Anna had wrapped themselves around one of his legs, Jacek and Przemek around the other, and Slavek was huggiung him around the waist. Bogdan,m the oldest, looked on laughing. Danuta came in and pried the children loose from Lech. In a few moments dinner was ready.

After dinner we retired to the living room to relax and recount the events of the day. There was mail that had been delivered, more packages, more food, even chocolate for the children.

"Does it ever go bad?" I asked.

"Hardly," Lech answered. "What we do not use is distributed to others or churches so that there is never any waste."

This was to be my last night with Lech. The evening passed quickly and we kissed and hugged one another before turning in. I thought that I might miss them both in the morning as I was getting up at 4:30 a.m. to start back to Warsaw for my flight home.

At 4:30 a.m. the next morning, I did get up and finished packing with as little noise as possible. I headed for the kitchen to make myself some tea and was startled to find Danuta at the stove, working quietly to surprise me. We sat down alone for a moment discussing how I might help her once I got back home to America by forwarding any goods that might be scarce or unavailable to her, or things I could send her for the children. A few minutes later, Lech surprised us both by walking in himself. We all had breakfast—eggs and sausage for the long journey ahead. Lech had decided to return to the city of Grudziadz because he had received news that Anna Walentynowicz's trial was to resume that day. In a few minutes, Maciej and Mietek were urging Lech to get ready to leave. There was a round of hugging and kissing again and I said goodbye as the three of them left. Through the kitchen window I could see them walkiung iun a slight rain to the van parked on the street below. Lech paused before getting in to examine a fresh "V" sign that had been smudged in the dust on the door of the van. He looked back toward me at the window, and flashed a "thumbs up" farewell. I watched the van drive up the street, wonderiung what awaited him that day, thinking perhaps, that it was all of Poland.

Wiktoria, Lerh, and Danuta play on the beach at Stogi.

A month after his release, Lech holds Wiktoria, who was born while he was in prison.

*Lech, Danuta, and three of the children
share a warm moment.*

My brother Hank prepares to give Danuta the traditional Polish hand kiss.

*Lech works in the makeshift office he has
set up in his kitchen.*

AFTERWORD

As you might expect, I have been asked fairly often to describe what Lech Walesa is "really like." I would hope that by this point in my story, after I have said what I can about it, that the reader will be able to see a good deal for himself of the Lech Walesa I became acquainted with on my visits. I would again express my reservation that I can not speak with the assurance of an expert as to what the answer to this question is. Nor can I speak for Lech himself on this question.

But, I can hazard a summary of impressions that I now have of him, impressions that my visits and conversations with him have served to confirm.

Lech Walesa is a man of strong faith.

He is someone who wants to help people and he does not mind putting himself out for others.

He is a man who knows what he wants but is willing to be reasonable and bide his time until he sees a realistic chance of achieving it.

He is a man who will not sell out. He is a family man with a deep devotion to his wife and children.

He is restless, rarely still, and a chain smoker. His reaction to any sudden event is almost always the expression, "Mama Mia," which is, I believe, the

*Lech looks at the "V'" sign of Solidarity
that someone has written on his van.*

extent of his knowledge of Italian. He does not like to pose for photographers but has always been willing to do so for what he thought was the good of the workers' movement. He knows very well the value of keeping the rest of the world aware of and interested in workers' events in Poland.

It is surprising to me that the Polish government has not made more concessions to him. He has the unusual talent of being able to combine a zeal for freedom and reform together with a reasonable sense of the realities and limits of the situation in Poland today. He is a charismatic figure who holds the attention of all sides. Although a devout Catholic, he does not impose his religion on anyone. He believes in the separation of church and state. One night I asked him if the church ever interferred with his union activity. "The church is doing its job, and I do mine. We have the same ideals and values— truth, justice, and honesty."

Of course, I treasure all of my own dealings with Lech, slight as they may be when measured against the forces and events he has had to face and will continue to face in his time. I willingly make whatever small contribution I may to help attain his goals.

But if there was ever a man to lead change, but reconcile it to existing realities, to rally the people of Poland to the support of new programs and more sacrifices, that man is Lech Walesa.

God bless you, Lech. As the pastor's mother said, "May you live a hundred years. Poland is not lost while you are with us."

The End

Lech Walesa sports his Solidarity pin.